LUCK,CHANCE & COINCIDENCE

A fascinating, entertaining and thought-provoking look at the effects of luck and coincidence, including ways in which this fickle phenomenon may be predicted, changed or improved.

G000136436

LUCK, CHANCE & COINCIDENCE

The Mysterious Power of Luck–and How to Make Yours Better

by

Steve Richards

THE AQUARIAN PRESS
Wellingborough, Northamptonshire

First published 1985

British Library Cataloguing in Publication Data

Richards, Steve
  Luck, chance and coincidence.
  1. Coincidence in psychical research—
  Case studies
  I. Title
  133.8   BF1175

  ISBN 0-85030-401-6

The Aquarian Press is part of the
Thorsons Publishing Group

Printed and bound in Great Britain

Acknowledgements

The author is grateful to the Association for Research and Enlightenment at P.O. Box 595, Virginia Beach, Virginia 23451 (USA) for permission to quote from their August 1983 Membership Research Project, 'Synchronicity and Consciousness', and to *The New York Times* for the story 'Sanitarium's Errors Kill a Frenchman', Copyrighted 1928 by The New York Times Company, reprinted by permission.

Contents

1

The Seventh Son of the Seventh Son

Trivial events can have the most astonishing consequences. Pascal is said to have remarked once that if Cleopatra's nose had been shorter, that alone would have changed the history of the world.[1] That may seem an exaggeration, but trivial events *do* shape history — a fact that has fascinated historians as far back as Livy.

Golda Meir's father was a Russian Jew who lived in the Tsarist empire before the Revolution, and who was moved by the intolerable anti-Semitism that existed there to emigrate to America. Ultimately, he settled in Minnesota and sent for his family to join him. Now this man was important to himself and to his family, but he was one of those simple folk whose doings tend not to be of great importance to the world at large. Yet, had he not decided to change addresses, the most monumental consequences would have ensued. His daughter received private tutoring in Russia, but it was not customary then for Russian girls to receive a formal education. Had she not received an advanced education it is conceivable that she might never have become a power in the Zionist movement, and had *that* not happened, she might never have become Prime Minister of the State of Israel. One could argue that the private decisions of a Russian carpenter literally changed the fate of the Arab world.

Perhaps even more significant is the story of the fellow who tried to kill Hitler. Early in Hitler's career, one of his associates became disenchanted with his movement for one reason or another and decided to kill him, which certainly would have been a laudable act. He planted a bomb close to where Hitler was supposed to stand and speak, but at a critical moment had to make a quick stop at that device which is known as a water closet or restroom, depending on where you happen to live. As he prepared to leave he discovered that someone had locked him in, and he was not able to escape until after Hitler had finished speaking. So it could be said that this seemingly trivial incident made possible the Holocaust and World War II. Moral — if you are ever entering one of these places and see someone in a hurry to get out, for God's sake, do not stand in his way![2]

In 1967 a man in New York found luck doing just the opposite — dawdling! He had been scheduled to take an air taxi to New York from New Jersey but, for one reason or another, he did not arrive with his usual promptitude. It was lucky for him that he did not. His plane took off without him, then crashed.[3]

Or what about this, from Alton, Illinois? Mrs Mildred West reported obituaries for the *Alton Evening Telegraph*, and even in Alton there were an average of ten deaths per week to report. Mrs West takes holidays, however, just as everyone else does and, when she went on a one-week holiday in 1946, the people of Alton obligingly stopped dying until she returned to her desk.[4]

Or this? A lady who gave birth to a son in a home for unmarried mothers in Australia met him again by accident ten years laters. He had been adopted by her fiancé![5]

This is the kind of stuff that luck is made of — strange, baffling coincidences which we all know are of course *just* coincidences, but which are so extraordinary that it is difficult to feel sure.

There is a minor coincidence in the fact that Germany capitulated to the Western Allies on 11 November 1918 at 11 a.m. which is to say, the eleventh hour of the eleventh day of the eleventh month of the year. It is also interesting to note the significance of the phrase 'eleventh hour' in this regard. Germany, at that moment, had reached the 'eleventh hour' in more ways than one.

Colonel Olcott, who is known to many as one of the Founders of the Theosophical Society, mentions a whole cluster of coincidences of this sort. In his *Old Diary Leaves* he points out that Madame Blavatsky 'arrived at New York on the 7th of July, 1873 — that is to say on the *seventh* day of the *seventh* month of her forty-second year [which is six times *seven*], and that our meeting was postponed until I should have attained *my* forty-second year [or six times *seven* again]. It must also be remarked that she died in the *seventh* month of the *seventeenth* year of our Theosophical relationship. Add to this the further fact, recently published by me in *The Theosophist*, that Mrs Annie Besant came to H.P.B. as an applicant for membership in the *seventh* month of the *seventeenth* year after her final withdrawal from the Christian communion, and we have here a pretty set of coincidences to bear in mind.'

Especially pretty when we remember that the Theosophists consider seven to be a sort of sacred number. Elsewhere, Olcott indicated that he believed this coincidence to be somehow more than a mere coincidence.

That is a trait that he shared with most of the human race. As Jung pointed out, when these coincidences go so far, they tend to acquire a 'numinous' quality. It becomes more difficult to believe that they just somehow happened. Something in us insists on believing that they are significant.'

Perhaps the classic tale of coincidence comes from Camille Flammarion's book, *L'Inconnu*, and concerns a neglected French poet named Emile Deschamps. 'In his childhood,' says Flammarion, 'being at a boarding school at Orléans, he chanced to find himself on a certain day at table with a M de Fortgibu, an émigré recently returned from England, who made him taste a plum pudding, a dish almost unknown at that time in France.' Ten years later as he walked past a restaurant on the Boulevard Poissonière, he chanced to spot 'a plum pudding of most excellent appearance.' He went inside, thinking to order it, but was told it had already been ordered – and by the very same M de Fortgibu. The memory of this incident never left him and, when he was invited to a dinner party many years later where 'a real English plum pudding' was to be served, he joked with the hostess that M de Fortgibu would surely join him. On the night in question the guests were hardly seated when the door opened and a servant announced that M de Fortgibu really *had* joined them. 'My hair stood up on my head,' wrote Deschamps. '[Mozart's] Don Juan . . . was not more terrified by his guest of stone.' The old gentleman 'had been asked to dinner by a friend who lived in the same house, but had mistaken the number of his apartment.'[6]

Astonishing as that is, Flammarion tells another tale which is even more interesting. It took place during the middle of summer, while Flammarion was in the study connected to his observatory, working on what he describes with becoming modesty as 'my great book on the atmosphere'. He had just completed one of the chapters when suddenly the wind rose, blew open a window on the southwest side of his study, and picked up all his papers, carrying them through the open window on the east side, and scattering them over the Avenue de l'Observatoire. Immediately thereafter it started to pour down with rain, making it useless to go out and search for the papers. It seemed to Flammarion that the entire chapter was lost, but a few days later he received proofs of that very same chapter from Lahure's printing house, and without a single page missing! Now this was remarkable enough, since Lahure's printing house was a full half mile from the observatory, and since one would not think the wind capable of operating a delivery service, but what *really* made the incident remarkable was the chapter's subject matter. *It had to do with the force of the wind.*

It would almost seem that the gods of wind and storm were so flattered to have such an eminent astronomer write about them that they wanted to get his remarks to the publisher as quickly as possible. But it transpired that there was a more mundane explanation. A porter connected with the printing office happened to live near the observatory, and on the way to work earlier that same day he had picked up some of Flammarion's papers to deliver to the typesetter. After the incident with the wind, the same porter happened by again, saw Flammarion's pages lying on the ground, and thought that he had dropped them earlier without realizing it. In order to keep from being reprimanded or even fired for his carelessness, he carefully sought out all the pages, arranged them in their correct order, delivered them to Lahure's, and saw to it they were properly typeset, even though the ink had been smeared by the rain. Most of all, he took care that nobody found out what had happened. One almost regrets that anyone ever *did* find out, but even so, it is still a good story.[7]

Wilhelm von Scholz tells of a woman who took a photograph of her son in the Black Forest, and had left the film in Strasbourg for developing, when the First World War broke out. There are perhaps worse things than war, but losing a roll of film is not one of them. The woman abandoned the film, and bought another roll in Frankfurt in 1916, *two years later.* She took a picture of her daugher with it, but when she had the film developed, it turned out to be double exposed. It was the very same roll she had left in Strasbourg in 1914, and the earlier image was the picture of her son.[8]

The next story is perhaps the most extraordinary coincidence of all — in fact it is *such* a coincidence that there are those who think it may signify some psychic phenomenon, and not be a coincidence at all. In 1837 Edgar Allen Poe wrote a mystery story called *The Narrative of Arthur Gordon Pym*, in which four men were shipwrecked and found themselves adrift in an open boat. They drew straws to decide which one of them should be killed and eaten by the other three, and the fatal straw was drawn by the cabin boy, Richard Parker.

Now what makes this interesting is that in 1884 this very thing actually happened. An English merchant vessel was shipwrecked, and four men were adrift in an open boat — just as it happened in Poe's story. The four drew straws to determine which of them should be killed and eaten — just as in Poe's story — and the loser was the cabin boy — again, just as in Poe's story. Moreover, *the unlucky cabin boy's name was Richard Parker!* It is ironic that, because Parker's shipmates elected not to die of starvation at sea, they died by hanging when they returned to England. A supreme case of bad luck if there ever was one.[9]

A century or so ago, astrologers used to quote the story of Samuel Hemmings as proof of the validity of astrology. Mr Hemmings was born on 4 June 1738, the same day as King George III. Moreover, he was born at *exactly the same moment* as the King, and in the same parish, which was St Martin's in the Fields.

This seems to have been the start of a series of coincidences which lasted throughout his life. Hemmings went into business for himself as an ironmonger in October 1760, just as George III was 'going into business for himself' by becoming King of Great Britain. He and the King married on the very same day, 8 September 1761. And there were 'other events of his life' according to his biographers which 'resembled those which happened to the late King.' One might think that these coincidences happened by design rather than by chance or astrological influence, but there was one which would have been difficult to pull off by design. Just as they had been born on the same day, Hemmings and George III died on the same day, Saturday 29 January 1820. J.M. Ashmand, who relates these events based on newspaper accounts published in February 1820, says that 'these coincidences are, at least, highly remarkable.'[10] One might think that the trade of ironmonger was perhaps less grandiose than that of being King, but Hemmings' biographers find a coincidence of sorts even here. Apparently, as ironmongers went in those days, he was quite prosperous, they say.[11]

In an interview with *The New York Times*, poet Carl Sandburg predicted that he would die at an age which would be a multiple of eleven years. 'I had two great-grandfathers and a grandfather who died in years divisible by eleven,' he said, and 'if I don't die at 88, I'll go on to 99.'[12] He was 80 when he first made this prediction, but he missed the boat by a few months. He died in his 89th year.

A coincidence which was pointed out by writer Ladislas Farago had to do with the so-called 'deadly double' advertisements which were placed in *The New Yorker* just sixteen days before the Japanese attack on Pearl Harbour. Ostensibly, the ads were supposed to sell a game called 'The Deadly Double', but Ladislas Farago, author of *The Broken Seal*, points out that within the ad can be found numbers and symbols which seem to indicate the date and hour of the attack. *New York Mirror* reporter Gordon Kahn, who first noticed the ads and their apparent significance, was apparently unable to find any evidence that 'The Deadly Double' had ever even been marketed as a game, and this led Farago to believe that the ads were placed covertly by Japanese agents, to warn their accomplices in New York that something was imminent.[13]

It turns out, however, that there really *was* a game by that name, and that the ads had nothing to do with the Pearl Harbour attack. The Japanese, after all, considered the details of this attack a state secret of the highest order. They were hardly inclined to publish those details in an American magazine, even covertly. The similarities between facets of the ad and historical incidents was nothing more than an amazing coincidence.

Arthur Koestler found that an even more strange set of coincidences materialized in England just before the invasion of Normandy. Four of the code words used in connection with the invasion were *Utah, Omaha, Mulberry,* and *Neptune,* and there was considerable anxiety about these words, because it was impossible to keep the Germans from figuring out that an invasion was imminent. Everything depended on keeping the sites where troops would land secret.

Even though Utah is not a word that logically should be on the lips of every Englishman, it turned up in a crossword puzzle that was published in the London *Daily Telegraph* for 3 May, 1944. Omaha appeared on the 23rd, Mulberry appeared on the 31st, and both Overlord and Neptune appeared on 2 June, just *four days* before the invasion was scheduled to commence. It should come as no surprise that the London *Daily Telegraph* soon received a visit from British Intelligence.

Once again, though, mere coincidence seems to have been at work. The man who designed these puzzles knew nothing about the invasion and selected the words with no knowledge of their significance. [14]

When Norman Mailer started his novel *Barbary Shore* it was entirely bereft of Russian spies. As the novel proceeded, however, a Russian spy began to appear in it, and eventually became the dominant character. When the novel was finished, real-life Russian spy Rudolph Abel was arrested by American counter-intelligence authorities. He lived in the same building as Mailer. [15]

Martin Gardner, who looks askance at these things, points out that not only is the Sun 400 times as large as the Moon, but it is 400 times as far away. [16] Mere coincidence, he says. Some coincidences, however, may point to previously undiscovered scientific truths. British physicist Paul Dirac has established a number of coincidences that have something to do with the number 10^{40}. Now 10^{40} is scientific shorthand for 10,000,000,000,000,000,000,000,000,000,000,000,000,000 — one followed by forty zeros — and it happens to be a number that recurs in all kinds of scientifically interesting places, although nobody knows why.

The largest obvious unit of space, for example, is the universe itself, whereas the smallest is an elementary particle, such as the electron. It happens that the universe is 10^{40} times as large as an electron. The largest obvious unit of time is the suspected 'age' of the universe, which is about 20 billion years, and the smallest unit of time is the *chronon*, which lasts 10^{-24} seconds. The universe is therefore 10^{40} chronons old. The electrostatic force between the nucleus of a hydrogen atom and its orbiting electron is 10^{40} times as powerful as the gravitational attraction between them. And the entire universe is 10^{80} times as heavy as a single hydrogen atom. 10^{80} is 10^{40} squared.

Some of Dirac's coincidences are a little more esoteric. He maintains, for instance, that the number of photons in the entire universe is greater than the total number of nuclear particles by a factor which is the *fourth root* of 10^{40}. Moreover, the size of an elementary particle is greater than the 'shortest length possible' by a factor which is the *square* root of 10^{40}.[17]

Apparently, some of Jung's 'numinous quality' has seized hold of the mind of Professor Dirac, for he does not believe that all these coincidences can be *mere* coincidences, and he may turn out to be right. After all, the modern theory of light originated with the 'coincidence' that electromagnetic waves propagate through space at the same velocity as light waves. That turned out *not* to be a coincidence. And Professor Dirac's 'coincidences' may turn out not to be coincidences, either.

But what about Poe's Richard Parker, or Deschamps' Monsieur de Fortgibu, or for that matter, the fellow who, out of thousands of gamblers, ends up with the winning number in the Irish Sweepstakes? They may all be coincidences, and then again they may not. But, as we shall see, there is no such thing as a *mere* coincidence. Even guaranteed meaningless concatenations of events have an underlying 'meaning' of sorts, if we know where to look for it, and they divulge some interesting mathematical and metaphysical laws.

2
Having Fun with Probability

There is a school of thought that is popular among modern scientists which holds that luck is *just* luck, and that coincidences are, as they say, *mere* coincidences. These folks are worth listening to for a number of reasons, but we should not treat them as oracles. There are some important strengths in their theory, but there are also some weaknesses which, in certain quarters, it is considered slightly impolite to talk about.

The strengths come from the fact that they have replaced the vague ways of thinking about luck that are common amongst laymen with precise, scientific ways. I believe it was Rod Serling who said that science fiction is the improbable made possible and fantasy the impossible made probable.[1] 'Very clever', the scientist would say. 'But what is impossible? And what is possible? And what is probable?'

One definition could be that the probable is just whatever we would expect, improbable is just whatever would surprise us, and impossible is just whatever would cause us to question our sanity. It is improbable that you will meet a two-headed unicorn on the way to work tomorrow morning, and it is rather likely that you will have to continue paying taxes. But how probable is it that Edgar Allen Poe would write an accurate story of an actual murder at sea many years before the fact? Or that you will succeed in business? Or win the Irish Sweepstakes? When we start asking questions like these, vague responses based on gut-level intuitions do not seem to be quite adequate. We need something better.

That is why, centuries ago, certain mathematicians started working on what is known today as the mathematics of probability. Instead of saying a thing is 'likely' or 'possible' or 'improbable' the way laymen do, these mathematicians worked out ways for putting precise values on likelihoods.

To do this, they start with two definite probability conditions: Impossible and Inevitable. These are useful because everybody agrees on what they are. Impossible *never* happens, and Inevitable *always* happens. Since we want to reduce likelihoods to numbers, we start out by assigning two arbitrary numbers to our two definite probability conditions. Thus, Inevitable has a probability of, let us say, one, and Impossible has a probability of zero. Everything that is neither Impossible nor Inevitable falls somewhere between one and zero by default.

There is one other way of expressing this which is popular among laymen, and that is to assign Inevitable a 100 per cent probability. Impossible remains zero. Either of these two ways of expressing oneself is equally legitimate, and they may be used interchangeably in this discussion.

That said, let me add that, in natural situations (as distinguished from artificial situations), one never encounters *either* Impossible *or* Inevitable. Of course it is Inevitable that someone will win the Irish Sweepstakes and it is Impossible that everybody will win. Of, if you assemble 367 people into a room, it is Inevitable that at least two of them will have the same birthdays (about which more anon). But there is a clearly artificial element in these situations. In nature, it seems to be Impossible that anything could be Inevitable, and Inevitable that nothing can be Impossible. Natural situations tend to fit in that fuzzy area between these two.

We could say that death is inevitable and that eternal life is impossible, but that is almost the only exception, and there are religious movements which question even that. Scientifically speaking, they are within their rights to do so. Of course, the fact that they are *within* their rights does not mean that they *are* right. It simply means that their position is not absurd.

There is a finite probability that a kettle, placed on a gas ring, will freeze instead of boil. The probability is small, to be sure, but it is not zero, and the event is therefore not impossible. In fact, there have been times when I have been *waiting* for a kettle to boil when I fully expected to *see* it freeze! It has not happened yet, but I shall keep you posted.

Or consider the sunrise. I have seen the run rise on schedule for 13,505 consecutive days so, on the basis of inductive reasoning, as well as my erudite (ahem!) knowledge of astronomy and physics. I can say that there is *close* to 100 per cent probability that the sun will rise tomorrow. Big news, eh? And yet the probability is not 100 per cent exactly. We *could* wake up tomorrow and the sun could be gone (although the probability is also close to 100 per cent that we will *not* wake up if it is). We can say that it is highly likely the sun will rise tomorrow. But we cannot say that it is certain. The probability of any natural phenomenon tends to be somewhere between one and zero.

Where between one and zero is the problem. In many cases the exact figure can be calculated although, as Camille Flammarion pointed out, in some real-life situations the complexity of the problem can be so huge as to embarrass the greatest mathematicians. That complexity forces most of us to get by on gut-level intuition, whether we are mathematically tutored or not.

Thus, gut-level intuition is important enough to have a name given it in the theory of probability. It is known as *moral certainty*. It is just a feeling that this or that is probable or improbable, and is therefore distinguished from *mathematical certainty*, which is based on precise calculations of the odds. Moral certainty is what we guide our lives by, whereas mathematical certainty gives the objective truth of things, and the gap between these two can be very great indeed.

Take this example from Camille Flammarion: 'a man thirty-five years old, in good health, who is exposed to no particular danger, has one chance in a hundred of dying before the end of the year, and one chance in three thousand that he may die within a fortnight.' Yet 'who is there,' asks the astronomer, 'who does not think that he is certain to live more than two weeks?' [2] Who indeed?

Or this from Jean Francois Steiner's shocking book *Treblinka*. Steiner believes that Hitler's SS troops prevented a widespread revolt among European Jews marked for extermination by convincing them that, whereas *some* Jews would be killed, some others (meaning themselves) would not. Hence, it made more sense according to one form of reasoning to play the odds and co-operate, rather than risk certain death by offering armed resistance. [3]

The classic way of showing just how wrong moral certainty can be is the so-called 'Birthday Problem'. Teachers of probability use this demonstration in their classrooms, and it has been a favourite with party-goers for some time. It works like this: There are three hundred and sixty-five days in a year, and every one of us was born on one of those. Hence, if you are at a party with twenty-two other people, what is the likelihood that two of you will have the same birthday? Bear in mind that you only have 23 people present and that there are 365 days on which any one of them could have been born.

Improbable? Unlikely? Do you get a vague, gut-level feeling that it is a bad bet? Well, if you do, you are wrong. With twenty-three people in the room (you and twenty-two others) the odds of two people having the same birthday are about even. And, with some simple arithmetic, we can prove it.

Let us simplify the problem by starting with only two people in the room — you and someone else. You were born on one day of the year, and there are 365 days in a year, so if we subtract your birthday from the year we have 364 days left. That means there are 364 days on which the other fellow could have been born so that both you and he would have different birthdays. And *that* means that the likelihood of you and some stranger having different birthdays is

$$\frac{364}{365}$$

If we subtract your birthday and the stranger's birthday from the year, we have 363 days left. And that means there are 363 possibilities for a third person to enter the room and have a different birthday from either of you. The likelihood of all three of you having different birthdays is therefore

$$\frac{364 \times 363}{365 \times 365}$$

If still a *fourth* person enters the room, the likelihood of all four of you having different birthdays is

$$\frac{364 \times 363 \times 362}{365 \times 365 \times 365}$$

And so on. Now, if we get very many people in the room, it

is obvious that the arithmetic becomes very cumbersome. Hence, I have calculated the likelihoods for larger crowds using a computer. Here are the results, rounded off for printing since the original numbers were calculated to sixteen decimal places:

Size of Crowd	Probability of a Match (%)	Size of Crowd	Probability of a Match (%)
2	.274	26	59.82
3	.82	27	62.68
4	1.63	28	65.44
5	2.71	29	68.09
6	4.04	30	70.63
7	5.62	31	73.04
8	7.43	32	75.33
9	9.46	33	77.49
10	11.69	34	79.53
11	14.11	35	81.43
12	16.7	36	83.21
13	19.44	37	84.87
14	22.31	38	86.4
15	25.29	39	87.82
16	28.36	40	89.12
17	31.5	41	90.31
18	34.69	42	91.4
19	37.9	43	92.39
20	41.14	44	93.28
21	44.36	45	94.09
22	47.57	46	94.82
23	50.73	47	95.47
24	53.83	48	96.05
25	56.86	49	96.57

You can see that the probability of two people having the same birthday passes the 50 per cent mark with only 23 people in the room. It passes the 90 per cent mark with 41 people in the room, and it passes the 99 per cent mark with 57 people in the room. With 100 people in the room, the probability that two will have the same birthday is 99.999969275 per cent, which expressed a different way comes to odds of three million, two hundred and fifty-four thousand, six hundred and eighty-eight to one. This is regarded as the mathematical equivalent of 'certainty', although even such astronomical odds to not exclude the alternative possibility.

In *The American Statistician*, right after an article on 'Inequalities of Expectations of Random Variables Derived by Monotonicity or Convexity', Edmund A. Gehan suggests an interesting variation on this. In his classes, he demonstrates this principle by having his students call out their birth dates one by one, and a match is usually found after only a few names. This, too, is contrary to what we might think, based on mere intuition and seat-of-the-pants reckoning, but Mr Gehan works out some imposing equations which show that it makes 'sense' — mathematically, at least.[4]

If there are one hundred people in the room, there is a 23 per cent chance that the second birthday called out will match with the birthday of someone else in the room. After that, the likelihood increases rapidly with each new date. The third student to call out his birth date increases the probability to 41.7 per cent, the sixth to 73.76 per cent, and the tenth to 90.66 per cent, with ninety people still left in the room!

With a much smaller class, say with 35 people in it, the odds are approximately even after nine dates have been called out, and we pass the 80 per cent mark with the twenty-ninth date.

People who play this game at parties usually use birth dates, but Mr Gehan points out that the same mathematical principles hold true for death dates as well, and here we get into some interesting coincidences indeed.

Of the American Presidents, both Fillmore and Taft died on 6 March — not a very startling coincidence. But Jefferson, Adams, and Monroe died on 4 July, and three deaths on the same day begins to leave us with some of Jung's 'numinous quality'. But that is not all. Two of these — Jefferson and Adams — not only died on the same day of the year, but they died on the same day in the *same* year. Moreover, it was the same day of the year on which both of them had signed the Declaration of Independence, and, even more than that, it was the fiftieth anniversary of the signing!

Applying this principle to British Prime Ministers, we find some of the same kinds of coincidences presenting themselves. Andrew Bonar Law died on 30 October 1823 and the Duke of Portland died 30 October 1809. And there are some cross coincidences such as the Earl of Derby, who died on 23 October 1869 and the Marquess of Salisbury, who was born on that same day, but in 1861. But the really interesting coincidences start with the Earl of Ripon, who was Viscount Goderich when he was Prime Minister in 1827. He died on 28 January 1859, which is the same day as the Earl of Aberdeen was born in 1784. But the day when Ripon was *born* — 1 November 1782 — is the same day as Spencer Perceval was born, only, of course, Perceval was born in 1762, and the day that Perceval *died*, 11 May 1812, is the same day of the year that the Earl of Chatham died, although of course Chatham's death was recorded in 1778.

Another variation on this was suggested by William Moser. He says that the odds are even that two people in a crowd of fourteen will have birthdays that are *either* the same *or* consecutive. In a group of seven, there is a 60 per cent chance of two people having birthdays within a week of each other, and in a group of four, there is a 70 per cent chance of two birthdays within a month of each other.[5] Once again, these facts, although mathematically beyond dispute, baffle our ordinary sense of intuition.

The Birthday Problem has even played a part in an important criminal case, and here we see how even our sense of *mathematical* certainty can be deceived.

In June 1964, at about midday, an elderly woman in San Pedro, California was mugged in an alley. Some time afterward, a witness saw a blonde woman with a pony tail run from the alley and jump in a yellow car which was driven by a bearded Negro man. On the strength of that 'evidence', a blonde, pony-tailed woman who happened to be married to a bearded Negro man who happened to own a yellow car was arrested, along with her husband, and the prosecutor used the laws of mathematics to persuade the jury that the pair were guilty.

His reasoning was this: The chance of a girl being blonde is, let us say, one in four. The chances of a car being yellow are, say, one in ten. The chances of the couple who happened to occupy the car being of mixed race are one in one thousand, and so on. Multiplying these 'probabilities' together, the prosecutor was able to 'prove' that the odds against any couple having all those characteristics were twelve million to one. Obviously, here was a very odd couple indeed, he argued, and they were therefore the couple who committed the crime.

A local professor of mathematics was called as an expert witness, and, faced with that kind of reasoning, the jury was overwhelmed. There was only one possible verdict, or so it seemed, and that verdict was guilty.[6]

Judge Raymond Sullivan of the California Supreme Court did not agree, though. He pointed out that none of the probability estimates had been proved 'even roughly accurate', and that the twelve million to one odds calculation had to be considered 'wild conjecture'. Moreover, there were problems with the way the odds were calculated, even assuming the data were correct. But the really interesting thing is that twelve million to one turns out not to be so conclusive when applied to a city as enormous as Los Angeles. Using logic similar to that used in the Birthday Problem, and accepting the prosecutor's own estimates of the odds, Judge Sullivan was able to show that the probability of there being at least one other couple somewhere in the city which consisted of a blonde pony-tailed woman and a bearded Negro man who owned a yellow car was *forty-one per cent*. Since the couple were convicted on no more than just that, the court ruled that they were entitled to a reversal of conviction. The prosecutor could of course motion for a new trial, but as *Time*, which reported the story, said, 'the odds are against it.'[7]

This is one of the ways in which probability theory can be unconsciously abused — using numbers to prove that something *could* not have happened by chance. Unfortunately, that is something that mathematics cannot prove.

In an article in *Annales des sciences psychiques*, Dariex 'proves' the veridicality of wraiths using an argument like this. For those of my readers who are perhaps not familiar with psychic phenomena, a wraith is a vision of a person who is dying. To qualify as a *genuine* wraith, the vision must be seen at the moment of death, or slightly before or after, and by some distant person who knows the dying person but who does not know for a fact that the dying person *is* a dying person. And to qualify as a *veridical* wraith, the person whose wraith is seen must actually be dying at the time of sighting. Non-veridical sightings undoubtedly occur, and some of these may even be wish-fulfillment fantasies. But these of course have no place in books on parapsychology. They tend to confuse the sceptical.

According to M Dariex, there is one hallucination for every two hundred and forty-eight persons, and there are twenty-two chances in a thousand that a given person will die in a given year. If we divide that by 365 we get the probability that the same person will die on a given day. Multiplying all of those together, we get the probability that a given veridical wraith sighting could be veridical by chance alone. Thus we have:

$$\frac{22}{248 \times 1000 \times 365}$$

And that works out to:

$$\frac{1}{4,114,546}$$

Or, in street language, odds of four million, one hundred and fourteen thousand, five hundred and forty-six to one against wraiths happening by chance alone. As Flammarion chooses to interpret it, 'the probability of real telepathic action is 4,114,546 times more probable than the hypothesis of fortuitous coincidence' and he concludes by saying that 'here are figures which have their own eloquence.'[8] Well said, and I may as well say here that I agree with him that wraiths are genuine psychic phenomena. But we cannot prove it with mathematics. There are several *billion* people in the world, and with odds of merely four million to one against such an occurrence happening by chance, there is room for a very large number of these sightings every single day without mathematically minded sceptics needing to feel any embarrassment. The Society for Psychical Research has not logged nearly that many sightings.

These calculations are only valid, though, if the wraith occurred twelve hours before or twelve hours after the death. If the time span is shorter, the odds against chance increase dramatically.

Let us consider the following case, which was reported in *Phantasms of the Living*:

Nicholas and Frederick, both employed in the same office, had been friends for eight years. They thought a great deal of each other. On Monday, 19 March 1883, when Frederick came to the office he complained of having suffered from indigestion. He went to consult a doctor, who told him that his liver was in a very bad state, and gave him some medicine. On Thursday he did not seem to be much better. Saturday he did not come to the office, and Nicholas learned that his friend had been examined by a physician, who advised him to rest for two or three days, but did not think anything serious was the matter. This same Saturday, towards evening, being seated in his chamber, Nicholas saw his friend sitting before him, dressed as usual. He particularly noticed his clothes — his hat had a black ribbon, his overcoat was unbuttoned, and he had a cane in his hand. The spectre fixed his eyes upon his friend, and then disappeared. This recalled to the mind of Nicholas the words of Job: 'A spirit passed before me and the hair of my flesh stood up.' At this moment he felt an icy chill, and his hair stood up on his head. Then he turned to his wife and asked her what time it was. 'Twelve minutes to nine,' she answered. Then he said, 'The reason I asked was that Frederick is dead. I have just seen him.' She tried to persuade him that this was only his imagination, but he assured her that the vision had been so distinctly impressed upon his brain that nothing could change his opinion.

The next day, Sunday, at three in the afternoon, Frederick's brother came to tell of his friend's death, which happened the night before about nine o'clock. [9]

This story was confirmed by Frederick's brother and by his wife. Flammarion says that 'there is no doubt that the death occurred in the twenty-five minutes that passed between twenty-five minutes to nine and nine o'clock,' meaning that there could not have been an interval or more than twelve minutes between the sighting and the actual death. He therefore displays to us the following reasoning concerning the mathematical significance of the event:

We have seen that the probability of death during a stated period of twenty-four hours is

$$\frac{1000}{22 \times 365}$$

for an adult of any age, but for men of forty-eight (which was the age of Frederick), [the probability of dying in any given year] is $135/1000$, the official figures given by the tables of mortality [in 1900]. We have, therefore, for the probability of death each day $1/2703.7$. During a period of time of twelve minutes, continued 120 times in the twenty-four hours, it would be 120 times less, and instead of

$$\frac{22}{248 \times 1000 \times 365}$$

[for the probability of a wraith being veridical] we shall have

$$\frac{135}{248 \times 1000 \times 365 \times 120}$$

Or

$$\frac{1}{804,622,216}$$

He therefore concludes that 'the probability of telepathic action, as compared with the probability of a fortuitous coincidence, is in the proportion of EIGHT HUNDRED AND FOUR MILLION, SIX HUNDRED AND TWENTY-TWO THOUSAND, TWO HUNDRED AND SIXTEEN TO ONE.' That is far more impressive than a few lousy million, but even so, it is less than a billion, and that leaves lots of room for chance.

Flammarion, however, thinks that 'we ought to feel satisfied with a probability of *several million*, because we must take into account cases where the person who died was known to be ill, and his friends might have been thinking of his death.'

Those of my readers who happen to believe that Jesus was the Messiah will be interested to know that even *that* seems to have been 'proved' mathematically – or at least the odds in favour have been calculated.

Credit for this one goes to a lady in Downers Grove, Illinois, just outside Chicago. In an article in the *Illinois Benedictine Magazine*, she contends that there were 332 prophecies in the Old Testament concerning the Messiah which were fulfilled in the case of Jesus. Estimating the probabilities for seven of them, she multiplied the numbers together, and estimated that the odds against Jesus *not* being the Messiah were 6,615,000,000,000,-000,000,000 to 1. After figuring probabilities for the other 325 prophecies and multiplying those in, the odds get *really* long. [10]

The odds against someone else fulfilling just a few of the 332 prophecies, though, are not so great, which may explain why there were so many others who thought *they* were the Messiah. One of the more improbable prophecies, that 'out of Judea should come one who would rule the world', was oddly fulfilled by Vespasian, who was in Judea when he was summoned to Rome, there to be crowned emperor. [11] He was not the Messiah, of course, because he was not only not Jewish, but he was working for the Opposition. And besides there were 331 *other* prophecies that were *not* fulfilled in his case.

There is a probability paradox which is similar to the Birthday Problem but is far less well known, and yet which is more astonishing. It is known as the 'Small World Problem'.

The 'Small World Problem' is a traveller's paradox. You are spending a holiday in Kuala Lumpur, let us say, and you run into someone there who knows an old schoolmate of yours whom you have not seen in twenty years. Arthur Koestler gives an actual example of this in *The Challenge of Chance*. A receptionist on holiday in Austria met an old friend of her boss, who was on holiday from Australia. On the same trip she met another friend of her boss, who was from South Africa. The boss, of course, lived in London.[12] These kinds of coincidence seem incredible when they occur, and yet they are much more probable than you might think.

Ithiel de Sola Pool of MIT and Manfred Hochen of IBM worked out mathematically that if each person in a country the size of the United States knows about 500 people at least casually, the odds against any two people knowing each other are about 200,000 to one. That agrees with what intuition would tell us. However, if we bring 'intermediaries' into the picture (in other words, if they do not know each other, but they both know some third person), the odds drop dramatically, just as they did with the Birthday Problem. In fact, the odds are better than even that *any* two people in the USA can be linked together by no more than *two* of these intermediaries. And this is out of a population of more than two hundred million people![13]

That seems impossible to believe, but psychologist Stanley Milgram put it to an experimental test, and discovered that the people in his sample could all be linked by an average of five intermediaries, despite the fact they lived in cities separated by hundreds of miles. He believes that more than two intermediaries were required because real-life social structures are more complicated than the ideal conditions proposed by the mathematicians.[14] Yet the Small World Problem is astonishing, nonetheless. And, in a country the size of Britain, it is not only possible but mathematically likely that there are no more than a few of these 'intermediaries' between any one of my readers and the Prime Minister, or even the Queen. A very small world indeed.

One way in which the Small World Problem works itself out is in family trees. If we are all descended from Adam and Eve, as many people still believe, then it is obvious that everyone in the world is distant cousin to everyone else in the world. (This happens to be true, by the way, whether you believe in the Adam and Eve myth or not. Adam and Eve only serve to make its reality more apparent.) Moreover, the number of links need not be as great as one might think. Just to give one famous example, three of the principal figures of the Second World War — Winston Churchill, Franklin Roosevelt, and General Douglas MacArthur — were all descended from a little-known lady from Taunton, Massachusetts named Sarah Barney Belcher. According to William Manchester, MacArthur was eighth cousin to Winston Churchill, and 'sixth cousin, once removed, of F.D.R.'[15]

A problem that fascinated the ancients was the probability of the writings of Homer being just a chance aggregation of Greek characters on a piece of parchment. In *De Divinatione*, Cicero uses this as an argument in favour of the existence of God. Homer's writings could not have just somehow happened by chance, he argues; so how much more unlikely is it that the universe, which is so much more wonderful, could have happened by chance?[16]

There are some flaws in that reasoning, but far be it from me to argue with Cicero. Suffice it to say that in our time we not only know that Homer's writings *could* be produced by chance — say, if you put a bunch of monkeys to banging away at typewriters — but we know about *how* probable it is.

Not very, you say? Well, there goes that gut-level thinking again. In his *Mathematician's Miscellany*, Littlewood works this problem out for Shakespeare's play *Hamlet*. If we suppose, he says, that there are 27,000 letters and spaces in the entire typescript of the play, and 35 keys on the typewriter, the odds against *Hamlet* resulting from a chance combination of key strokes are $35^{27,000}$ to 1.[17] Those are long odds, but it is not impossible. There is a finite likelihood that a group of monkeys *could* write *Hamlet* entirely by chance. But of course they would crank out a lot of penny dreadfuls and detective stories first.

Here, though, the laws of probability seem to support Cicero. According to Alan Vaughan, if a monkey typed ten characters per second, 'and we allow no banana breaks', it would take him about twenty billion years to type 'To be or not'. To get another 'to be' added to the end of that would require an additional ten billion monkeys typing for an additional twenty billion years![17] It is not impossible, of course, and materialistically-oriented scientists insist that it actually happened — the universe just somehow got here by chance. But in this instance the odds are getting long enough that something approaching genuine certainty seems to have been arrived at. If I had worked out the number $35\,^{27,000}$ (which I had originally intended to do), it would take the space allotted for this chapter to contain it. Those are long odds indeed.

We also get very long odds calculating the likelihood of there being snowballs in Hell or life on other planets. But where ordinary, day-to-day occurrences are concerned, the probabilities tend to be much smaller, and as Littlewood pointed out, odds of a million to one against are not so great if you have an entire lifetime for an interesting coincidence to take place.

The odds against being killed by lightning are about three million to one, but according to *Colliers Encyclopedia*, several hundred people are killed by lightning every year, nonetheless.[18] Standing in the open air strikes me as a strange way to try to commit suicide, but even if the odds against it are long, it is not impossible that the trick could work.

Camille Flammarion says that lightning struck a man in an open field without harming him in any way, except to remove his shoes, which were flung twenty feet away. He probably needed a new pair anyway.

Slightly less fortunate was a young peasant girl who was struck by lightning, just as the first fellow was, who was standing in an open field when it happened, just as the first fellow was, and who was completely unharmed, once again just as was the first fellow. Only in this instance, instead of merely losing her shoes, she seems to have lost everything. She was left lying on the ground completely naked — or so says Camille Flammarion — and her clothes were found neatly deposited in a nearby tree.

I am not so certain that I believe that last one, but his third story is both believable and grotesque. It is an instance of bad luck. A labourer was struck by lightning while he was eating his breakfast, just as he was about to lift a piece of bread into his mouth. This man was killed, and his body was left frozen in the position he had assumed when he died, with the bread still in his hand, and with his hand still lifted to his mouth. But what was remarkable about this was that, as soon as the body was touched, it immediately crumbled into ashes. And this time it was the clothes that were left unharmed.[19]

A man who was knocked out for twenty minutes by a lightning bolt in June 1981 discovered that lightning can be man's best friend. His hearing aid was destroyed by the blast, but that was no problem, because his hearing had somehow been restored to normal. His glasses were knocked off, but that was no problem either. He had been practically blind before the blast, but the lightning left him with twenty-twenty vision. Moreover, although he had been bald for 35 years, he now has a full head of hair. Unfortunately, according to Dean Havron, who reported the story, he was standing under a tree when the incident occurred, and it was not so fortunate. 'It's dying,' he says.[20]

Billy Bee to the contrary, lightning refuses to leave some people alone.* According to the *Guinness Book of World Records*, Roy C. Sullivan was struck seven times. He was a U.S. Park Ranger in Virginia, and became known as 'the human lightning conductor' because of his strange experiences. He lost his big toe nail in 1942 due to lightning, then was struck again in 1969, when his eyebrows were burned off. In 1970 lightning seared his shoulder, and in 1972 it set his hair on fire. He was struck again in 1973, again in 1976,and again in 1977. There is gruesome irony in the fact that after surviving all this he died in 1982 — by his own hand![22]

In medieval Europe people would have thought that the Deity was trying to tell him something. Chance events have been thought to be the work of the gods all the way back to ancient times. This belief is held by some people to this day — and lightning especially was thought to be the favourite instrument of divine wrath.

In some instances, this belief seems to have been curiously vindicated — or so it would appear. In Germany, in the eighteenth century, a Protestant clergyman named Lange was struck and killed by lightning, which aroused considerable suspicion among his countrymen. Those suspicions were further aroused when his body was being prepared for burial. Sewed into his clothes were found secret papers which identified Lange as a member

* Billy Bee is the one who said that 'lightning never strikes twice in the same . . .'[21]

of a secret anti-monarchical society called the Illuminati. This discovery led to numerous arrests and the suppression of the society, although the possibility of its continued existence disturbs the serenity of conspiracy-oriented ultra-rightists to this day.

Because of this belief, Benjamin Franklin was thought impious for inventing his lightning rods, and when the great earthquake of 1755 shook Massachusetts, the Reverend Thomas Prince of the Old South Church suggested that God had found a new way of expressing his wrath. He had studied the matter statistically, and discovered that there was an increase in the frequency of earthquakes after lightning rods had started to be deployed. Probability theorists would call it a 'statistically meaningful correlation'.

Franklin lived in Boston and, as the Reverend pointed out, 'in Boston are more [lightning rods] erected than anywhere else in New England, and Boston seems to be more dreadfully shaken. Oh!', he lamented, 'there is no getting out of the mighty hand of God'.[23]

I have quoted this because it seems to be another example of how mathematics can lead to curious, and perhaps even invalid, conclusions. Mathematically, the Reverend was probably right. However, it seems logically outrageous that he would posit the existence of a Being who created the Heavens and the Earth, but who is completely stymied by 'the sagacious Mr Franklin' and his 'iron points'.

The probability of lightning striking certain kinds of structures is greater than for others, and the probability seems to be highest for structures which extend high into the air and are pointed — like church steeples. There is curious irony in this because it means that church steeples are more likely to be hit — a fact which has proved true historically and which has led to much theological controversy.

Before the natural laws which govern this phenomenon were understood, it was assumed that churches were more likely to be struck because of the malice of the 'Prince of the Powers of the Air', which is an archaic way of saying Satan. But even after the invention of the lightning rod, it was thought inappropriate to protect sacred buildings with the impious invention of Mr Franklin. Nowhere was resistance greater than in the city of Venice.

'In spite of the angel at its summit, and the bells consecrated to ward off the powers of the air, and the relics in the cathedral hard by, and the processions in the adjacent square, the Tower [of Saint Mark's] was frequently injured,' says White, 'and even ruined by lightning. In 1388 it was badly shattered; in 1417 and again in 1489 the wooden spire surmounting it was utterly consumed; it was again greatly injured in 1548, 1565, [and] 1653, and in 1745 it was struck so powerfully that the whole tower, which had been rebuilt of stone and brick, was shattered in thirty-seven places.'

Beccaria introduced Franklin's lightning rods into Italy, but the faithful did not want to desecrate their cathedral with such a heathen invention. Unprotected, the Tower of Saint Mark's was struck again in 1761 and again in 1762.

This story illustrates another luck phenomenon which deserves a chapter all to itself: the fact that luck runs. The Tower of Saint Mark's was clearly on a run of the wrong sort. But the solution was simple enough. In 1766 a lightning rod was installed in the Tower according to White 'and it has never been struck since.' As we shall see, some other runs are not so easily manipulated.

3

Does Luck Run?

'And I looked, and I saw under the sun that the race is not to the swift, nor the battle to the strong, nor yet counsel to the wise, nor yet riches to men of skill, nor yet favour to men of understanding, but time and chance happeneth to them all.'
— *Ecclesiastes*

To the unaided sight, it appeared to be an ordinary Amtrak Silver Meteor on a routine trip from Miami to New York. But to officials of the National Transportation Safety Board, which oversees these things, it was the *Rogue Train.*

At 7.40 p.m. on Wednesday evening, 24 August 1983, in Savannah, Georgia, the Rogue Train struck and killed a woman who was fishing from a trestle. The necessary investigations were made, and the Rogue Train took off again.

At 9.30 p.m., less than two hours later that same evening, it destroyed a pickup truck in Ridgeland, South Carolina that was parked too close to the tracks. This second accident occurred barely sixteen miles from the first. The crew was replaced and the Rogue Train took off again.

At 1.10 a.m. Thursday, the Rogue Train hit a tractor-trailer at a grade crossing in Rowland, North Carolina. The driver was uninjured, but the train's engine and two passenger cars were derailed, sending 21 people to hospital. Despite these unfortunate accidents, the trains obviously had to keep rolling, and the Rogue Train took off again!

At 2.33 a.m. Friday, at Kenly, North Carolina, on the return trip from New York to Miami, the Rogue Train collided with a car, sending its driver to hospital with head injuries. According to the police, the driver ignored warning lights and sped over the tracks, right into the path of the train.

Now it must be emphasized that there was absolutely no question of fault on the part of the crews. According to investigators, both of the crews of this train obeyed all the normal procedures and safety precautions. What we have here is just an extraordinary run of bad luck.

The novelist Gilbert Patton had what, for a writer, must have been an extraordinary run of good luck. When he died in 1946 it transpired that he had written and successfully sold one dime novel every week for nine hundred and eighty-six consecutive weeks.[1]

A 'run' of a different sort came to an end not so long ago for the New York Yacht Club when they lost the America's Cup to the Royal Perth Yacht Club in Australia. They had hitherto defended this rather unattractive ornament against all comers — mostly British — for an amazing 132 years. This had been the longest run of luck enjoyed by any sporting organization in any sport in history.

In 1950, according to the *New York Herald Tribune*, an unidentified man walked up to a crap table in a Las Vegas casino called the 'Desert Inn' and monopolized the dice for an hour and twenty minutes, during which he made his point an astonishing twenty-eight consecutive times. The odds against this were calculated by someone at the casino as approximately ten million to one.

The odds against the Desert Inn remaining financially solvent would have been even worse if the man had re-bet his entire stake on every throw of the dice. As it happened, he never risked more than $50 on a single throw, pocketing the rest of his money after every win. When he eventually lost — on the twenty-ninth throw of the dice — he had won $750. Side bettors who were less conservative walked away with a staggering one-hundred and fifty-thousand dollars![2] If the Rogue Train had a run of bad luck, this fellow had a run of good.

In his *Strange Lives of One Man*, Ely Culbertson tells a presumably true story of a run that happened his way while he was playing roulette. He had just placed a bet on red, but got into an argument with another gentleman before the wheel stopped spinning. He left his bet on the table, escorted the gentleman outside the casino where the disagreement could be settled in private, and returned to his table after a considerable time to discover that his original bet was still on the table and still winning![3]

In February of 1928 two sisters named Dolly won $850,000 at a casino in Cannes, France, which was on a run of the wrong kind. The Greek syndicate which owned the casino reported that it had lost thirty million francs during the Winter Season, the worst losses they had suffered in eight years.

Casinos are a zero sum game, though, and what is bad for the owners is good for the customers. One of the Dolly sisters, the wife of a Canadian tobacco heir, won 4 million francs just after midnight, and was ahead by 5.5 million francs before the night was over. The casino had lost ten consecutive times in three hours.[4]

Camille Flammarion mentions a similar occurrence at a roulette table at Monte Carlo. He says that the same number came up five times running and that red has been known to come up 21 times in succession. The odds against this have been calculated as two million to one.[5] The longest run in Monte Carlo history was reported by Warren Weaver, author of *Lady Luck*. Red came up twenty-eight times in a row, beating Flammarion's record by seven. Since we have a geometric progression here, the odds against this are considerably greater than against Flammarion's shorter run. According to Weaver's calculations, they are about 270 million to one.[6]

The opportunities presented by a run like this are tantalizing to contemplate. According to Flammarion, had a gambler bet 1 louis, he would have won 35 louis, or 700 francs, on the first win. Had he left the same sum on the table, the second time the number came up he would have won 24,500 francs. This is known as parlaying your winnings. On the third win he would have had an amazing 857,000 francs, but — alas! — according to the French astronomer, 'the rules of the bank will not permit this; they fix the maximum of the stake at 9 louis. The bank allows no gain greater than 120,000 francs.'[7] Of course, that was written at the turn of the century, and the rules have changed since then, but all casinos still protect themselves in some such manner. Their object is to put *you* out of business; not to bankrupt themselves.

If this were not done, all the casinos in the world could be beaten with a simple technique known as the Martingale.

With the Martingale, you do not need a run of good luck. You simply start out betting a single pound, and each time you lose, you double your bet. When you win — and you surely will if you play long enough — you recover all your losses, plus one pound in profits. However, to come out ahead, you have to keep doubling those bets, and the size of your bet grows very large very quickly, meaning that you are either going to exceed the house limit, or you are going to run out of money. This is the phenomenon known in the theory of probability as 'gambler's ruin', and as usual the probability folks scoff at any idea that runs of luck could have any meaning.[8]

To the probability people, runs of luck are just mere chance events. In fact, in their *Statistical Tables*, Rohlf and Sokal have worked out actual numbers whereby a run of luck can be tested, to *prove* that it occurs by mere chance.[9] If the number of runs is less than or equal to a certain critical value which can be established by the table, it is random — or so say the mathematicians.

For all that, though, there is a school of thought which holds that runs of luck are *not* chance occurrences, and the High Priest and Chief Apostle of that school is a German biologist named Paul Kammerer.

Kammerer was the author of *Das Gesetz der Serie*, which means *The Law of Series* in English, and he thought that runs of luck were meaningful events. More than that, he thought runs could be explained by all sorts of strange new laws. He wrote in his book that runs were 'a simple empirical fact which has to be accepted and which cannot be explained by coincidence — or rather, which makes coincidence rule to such an extent that the concept of coincidence itself is negated.[10] As a biologist, he seems to have even believed that runs could be classified, like one of his frogs.

Here is one of Kammerer's examples: an anecdote which figures in his classification system as a 'series of the third order':

On 28 July 1915, Kammerer's wife read a novel by Hermann Bang which contained a character named 'Mrs Rohan'. Later in the day, at a tram station, she saw a man who looked just like Prince Josef Rohan, who happened to be a friend of hers. Later that evening, she was visited by the *real* Prince Rohan, who thereby furnished the third element in the series. But that is not all.

Earlier in the day, while she was in the tram station standing close to the man who resembled Prince Rohan, she overheard someone mention the village of Weissenbach on Lake Attersee and ask if it were a pleasant place for a holiday. After leaving the tram, she went to a delicatessen on the Naschmarkt, and was asked by the attendant if she knew the village of Weissenbach on Lake Attersee. He had to make a delivery by mail and did not know how to address his parcel. [11]

This reminds me of a story told by Littlewood in his *Mathematician's Miscellany*. A girl wanted to visit her sister, whose name happened to be Florence Rose Dalton, and who worked as a servant at 42 Walton Street, in London. The girl was not familiar with the neighbourhood and, in trying to find number 42, somehow managed to get off Walton Street and onto Ovington Square without realizing it. She arrived at 42 Ovington Square, thinking she was in fact at 42 Walton Street, knocked on the door, and was told that, yes, there was a Florence Rose Dalton working there, but that she was gone for two weeks holiday, and that *her* sister was standing in for her. Both of these ladies were named Florence Rose Dalton, both were servants, and both worked at the houses numbered 42 on two different streets which closely adjoined each other in the same city! Even Littlewood, who frankly admitted that he enjoyed 'debunking' these kinds of coincidences, regarded this story as 'genuinely remarkable.' [12]

In a few cases, runs of luck can be 'explained', although I dare say the explanation may not be satisfactory to everyone. In *The Challenge of Chance*, Arthur Koestler tells the story of a Bavarian lady who was apparently responsible for producing some poltergeist phenomena. I probably do not have to tell my readers that 'poltergeist' is a German word meaning, literally, 'noisy ghost'. The victim was a Dr Sigismund Adam of Rosenheim, a town near the Austrian Border. At first his telephone began behaving strangely, then the neon lights in his house were affected. In due course, electrical experts were called in, who disconnected Dr Adam's house from the local power supply net, and fixed him up with his own generator. This device had several meters installed with it, which recorded violent electrical changes whenever certain kinds of poltergeist activity were noticed in the house. In time, the disturbances were traced to an eighteen-year-old secretary, who was dismissed, with the result that the problems ceased.[13]

Now what makes this interesting is that this young lady apparently had the ability to unconsciously affect electrical devices. According to Koestler, she lost her fiancé because whenever he took her bowling (bowling was a passion of his that she did not share), the electrical system which controlled the bowling pins started breaking down.[14] I say this is interesting because, if it is true, it explains some run-of-luck type phenomena which are well known to every electrical engineer.

Any engineer can tell you that when a project deadline date nears, and tension builds among the design team as they race to produce something workable before the customer shows up to inspect it, things start going wrong with their instruments. This is always mentioned jokingly as just an example of Murphy's Law in action, but I have suspected for some time that these very delicate devices may be subject to being affected by psychic energy in a way that a less delicate device, such as a mechanical contraption, is not.

In illustration of this, let me share one of my own experiences with you. It took place on a Friday afternoon. Now Friday is for most of us the most trying part of the week anyway, and this particular Friday was particularly trying for me, for reasons which I have since forgotten. Hence, we have the phenomenon of emotional tension in someone surrounded with electrical instruments. Perhaps it was coincidence, and perhaps it was causality, but if I turned on, say, an oscilloscope, to work with it, the device immediately went on the blink. This was repeated with first one, then another of these instruments, until finally all the oscilloscopes we *had* were headed for the repair shop. There were still two or three hours left in the day, though, and to keep the afternoon from being a total loss, I decided to devote the time to some problems I had been working out on the company computer. We had a time-sharing terminal which connected us to an 1108 several miles away. Yet somehow I could not seem to get my jobs to run successfully. The following Monday, I was told that all fourteen tape drives in the system downtown had blown out simultaneously, that in some manner they had failed so as to affect only me and one other user, and that the failure was of such a nature as to elude the diagnostic programs used by the maintenance people to check on their electrical 'health'. The odds against that must be astronomical. To top everything else, a representative from the company which owned the computer was sent by to explain matters and to adjust our bill, since we were not to be charged for time on a computer that did not work, and the representative had the very same first and last name as another engineer I knew. I will not give his name out of respect for his privacy, but both his first and last names were most unusual, and this is the only time in a lifetime I have ever encountered anyone who shared either one of them with him.

These kinds of runs are trivial, though. In some cases runs of luck are not trivial at all, and can last an entire lifetime. You may regard Winston Churchill as a lucky man, but the first sixty years of his life were an extraordinary and protracted run of bad luck.

He was born prematurely. He failed at Harrow, then failed twice to win admission to Sandhurst. Once in, he was relegated to the cavalry, having failed to get into the more prestigious infantry regiments. He barely won his commission, and failed to win promotion after that. In South Africa he was captured by the Boers and interned in a concentration camp.[15]

Once in the government he failed to win elections, then, in the Admiralty, he was responsible for the disastrous expeditions to the Dardanelles and then to Gallipoli. As Chancellor of the Exchequer he played a major role in returning Britain to the gold standard, a move which led to deflation, unemployment, a miner's strike, and finally to the general strike of 1926. In 1939 he was responsible for losing Norway to the Germans. When he was named Prime Minister of Great Britain in 1940 he was well over sixty years old, and considered a brilliant loser. But his problems did not end there. Almost his first act of office was to preside over the disaster that overtook the British Expeditionary Force in Belgium and forcing them to abandon all their equipment and flee for their lives to Dunquerque. This disaster was followed by eighteen months of defeats in Africa, in Europe, and in the Far East — a period during which he had to suspend elections to stay in office. Any less determined man would have been altogether discouraged by this. Yet in 1942, after the Battle of Alamein, Churchill's luck turned, and an unbroken series of defeats gave way to an almost unbroken series of victories, which resulted in the collapse of all the Axis Powers in 1945. As he said himself the Battle of Alamein 'marked in fact the turning of the "Hinge of Fate". It may almost be said, "Before Alamein we never had a victory. After Alamein we never had a defeat." '[16] One run of luck had given way to another. But his luck did not end there. It was followed by a dazzling series of successes which left him a wealthy man, a Nobel Prize winner, a literary celebrity, and a member of the Order of the Garter.

Students of this elusive phenomenon suspect that Churchill's story may illustrate what we might call 'Run's First Law', which was formulated many years ago in three words:

'SUCCESS BREEDS SUCCESS'.

The corollary to that is of course that failure breeds failure. In general terms we might say that luck breeds luck, *whatever* kind it is. There is no doubt that talent is important, but Churchill had plenty of talent. The important thing may be to get some kind of luck 'momentum' going, and let it carry you from success to success.

We can see this run-of-luck phenomenon not only in the lives of individuals, but in whole countries. Unless we are going to assume that people in one country have substantially higher IQs than people in others — a premise which has been studied and proved to be wrong — there is no question that the success enjoyed by the world's more successful societies is a run of excellent luck. However much genius was involved, there is little doubt that a run of luck was indispensable for the successful conquest of the British Empire, and I suspect the same thing, working in the opposite direction, may have led to its decline. How could we explain the long decadence of the Chinese people, surely one of the most gifted and ingenious, not to say industrious, peoples in the world, if not by a run of bad luck? We are almost tempted to believe Kammerer's assertion that luck is controlled by a mysterious force in the universe which is as fundamental as gravity, and which draws together events the same way as gravity draws together chunks of matter.[17]

It is an intriguing hypothesis. But there are some unacknowledged debts in Kammerer's theory which even Arthur Koestler seems not to have noticed. And those debts can give us some practical insights into improving our luck.

4

But What About the Stock Market?

'October. This is one of the peculiarly dangerous months to speculate in stocks in. The others are July, January, September, April, November, May, March, June, December, August, and February.'

— Mark Twain, *Pudd'nhead Wilson*[1]

One thing left discreetly unmentioned in Kammerer's theories, and which not a single one of his commentators seems to have noticed, is that they were all rehashed theories about the behaviour of the stock market. Even Einstein was fooled. He is said to have remarked that Kammerer's theories were 'original and by no means absurd', but for once in his life he was no more than half right.[2] They were 'by no means absurd' to be sure, but original they were not.

There are two theoretical pillars of Kammerer's book: his theory of backward causation and his theory of 'inertia', and when he was around there were precisely two major schools of thought about how to make money speculating in the stock market. Each of Kammerer's two major theories about runs of luck is the theoretical basis for one of these two schools of stock speculation.

Consider his theory of 'backward causation', which looks at first like one of his more unusual theories. Backward causation means that something which is *going* to happen in the future (but has not happened yet) somehow determines something which *is* happening in the present. It is just the opposite of the more usual concept of causation, which is that things that *are* happening in the present affect what is *going* to happen in the future. Backward causation would certainly strike a physicist like Einstein as 'by no means absurd' because of the peculiar nature of time. Just to give one example, scientists have developed a new laser which is based on light waves which apparently travel backward in time. While we are coming out of the past and as it were disappearing into the future, these light waves come out of our future and disappear into our past. They pass us going in the opposite direction as it were. But backward causation is by no means unknown to stock market theorists. In fact, it is the basis for the so-called Fundamental school of stock speculation.

The Fundamental approach has to do with the nuts and bolts of what makes a company run: what new products they are planning to produce, whether they are acquiring other firms (or being acquired themselves), and such esoteric matters as debt/equity ratio, book value, percentage of retained earnings, and whatnot. By studying things of this kind, the Fundamentalist believes he can spot what he calls *intrinsic value* – a metaphysical something-or-other which may have nothing to do with the price of a stock right at this moment, but which conceivably could affect its long-term prospects.

Fundamentalists do not like to talk about it, but the rationale behind this approach is a variation on Kammerer's backward causation theory. Take the following statement from *The Money Game*, Adam Smith's book on the stock market. Discussing a widely shared belief about stock prices, Smith insists that 'in the long run, future earnings influence present values.'[3] In other words, a company's future profits, which are altogether unpredictable, somehow determine, or at least affect, the present price of the company's stock. If Smith is right – and he is not alone in his opinion – something which has not happened yet and which cannot be predicted is somehow 'causing' things to happen in the present. That is Kammerer's theory of backward causation. Or how about the notion that stock prices are a 'leading indicator' of economic performance. If the economy is going to go sour nine to twelve months from now, some stock analysts believe that 'causes' a depression in the stock market in the present. Likewise, if the economy is going to boom a year from now, that is believed to 'cause' a stock market boom in the present.[4] That is a backward causation theory, too. Nobody can predict these booms and busts, so the 'leading indicator' theory cannot be justified on psychological grounds. If it is true, it would seem that the boom in the future must be 'causing' stock prices to rise in the present.

The Technical approach has to do with the track record of the stock itself. Whereas the Fundamentalist concentrates on the company behind the stock, the Technician concentrates on what the stock is selling for, and on how the current price of a stock compares with its price yesterday and the day before.

If the stock's price has gone up the past few days, the Technician assumes that there is a tendency for it to *continue* going up — and that is a stock market version of Kammerer's inertia. The same thing is assumed on the way down. The Technician can be as esoteric as the Fundamentalist, however, and he spices his language with such ideas as 'heads and shoulders formations', 'double tops', 'line formations', 'reversals', and so on, which describe different patterns he sees as he charts the prices of his stocks from day to day. There is something to be said for both of these approaches, and there is a group of college professors who believe they know exactly what to say about both of them: they say that they are both eyewash.

These folks claim that stock prices follow what they call a *random walk*. What that means is that the price of a stock today has nothing to do with its price yesterday. And you can forget about such ideas as 'retained earnings' and 'debt/equity ratios', because all that is irrelevant, too. At any moment there is a fifty per cent probability that a stock will go up in price, and there is fifty per cent probability that it will go down.

In other words, it is like tossing a coin.

According to Professor Fama: 'the past history of the series [of stock price changes] cannot be used to predict the future in any meaningful way. The future path of the price level of a security is no more predictable than the path of a series of cumulated random numbers'.[5] The fact that a stock has been going up the past three or four days does not in any way signify that it will *continue* going up. You may flip seven heads in a row, but that does not tell you anything about the next toss of the coin. No matter how many times you toss, there is still a fifty-fifty chance of heads, and ditto for tails.

Now I think you can see how silly it is to try to 'analyse' a phenomenon like this by poring over a chart with a ruler in your hand, looking for 'heads and shoulders' formations, or by watching political events, or calculating book values, or scouting around for 'hot tips'.

In fact, it has been proved that with a fistful of darts you have about as much chance as a highly paid Wall Street Analyst of predicting which way the coin toss will go next. In fact, Senator Thomas McIntyre of the Senate Banking Committee did just that.

Senator McIntyre's committee was considering legislation to regulate the American mutual funds industry. A series of hearings were held, and several prominent economists, including Professor Paul Samuelson, introduced the committee members to the random walk theory of stock prices.

Senator McIntyre returned to his office, tacked the stock market page of the *New York Times* to his dart board, threw a few darts at it, and selected a portfolio that out-performed most of the mutual funds he proposed to regulate.[6] And he is not the only one.

In 1967 three officers of *Forbes* magazine selected a portfolio of twenty-eight stocks in exactly the same way as Senator McIntyre. Six years later, in 1973, their 'Dart Board Fund' had appreciated fourteen per cent, beating the Dow Jones Industrial Average, which had only gained five per cent over the same period and trouncing the Value Line 1400 Stock Index, which lost forty per cent of its value over the same period.[7] By 1982 their portfolio had appreciated 239 per cent in value. The Standard and Poor's index of 500 blue chip stocks rose thirty-five per cent over the same period of time.[8]

In an even more astonishing experiment, a financial consulting firm in Maryland called Computer Directions Advisers, Inc., programmed their computer to choose 100 portfolios, each comprising twenty-five stocks selected completely at random. Eighty-two of these portfolios outperformed the Standard and Poor's 500 throughout the ten years between 1967 and 1976, and ninety-nine of them beat the index in the final year of the test.[9] Moreover, according to the *Wall Street Journal*, three out of four mutual funds — run by highly paid, full-time professional stock analysts — failed to do as well as the market average throughout the entire period between 1967 and 1977. The study was done by Rogers, Casey, and Barksdale for the pension fund journal *Pensions and Investments*. They studied 141 pooled equity funds and 126 fixed income funds managed by banks and insurance companies. The pooled funds managed a $9.7 billion portfolio and the fixed income funds had $5.4 billion, so we are not talking about small investors here. The poorest performance was shown by one fund which consistently lost nine per cent a year throughout the entire time period between 1967 and 1977, and the *average* performance was a 3.5 per cent gain. By way of contrast, between 31 December 1974 and 1976 the stock market average gained sixty per cent and what is *really* discouraging is that ninety-day T-bills, which involve no risk whatever, averaged a 5.9 per cent return in the same time period, beating the funds managers by a full percentage point.[10] The magazine *Changing Times* reports that *eighty* to *eighty-five* per cent of all mutual funds do more poorly than the market.[11] No matter how much sophisticated rhetoric you cover the fact up with — and some of the rhetoric I have seen is very sophisticated indeed — the fact remains that stock prices are just successive flips of a coin. They are a random walk.

It is not surprising that this kind of thinking is anathema to stock analysts and brokers, but what may be surprising is that even some economists have had trouble accepting it. As late as the nineteen-thirties John Maynard Keynes insisted that the random walk theory, which he rather pompously described as 'the assumption of arithmetically equal probabilities based on a state of ignorance', could not be true because it 'leads to absurdities'.[12] The question is an empirical one, however, and not a philosophical one, and the empirical evidence has become so overwhelming today that most economists *do* accept it.

For that development we have to thank Professor James Lorie, who is considered by some 'the father of modern random-walk analysis'.[13] In 1964 Professor Lorie co-authored a paper entitled *Rates of Return on Investments in Common Stocks*, which contained the first extensive statistical proof that stock prices move up and down randomly. As the editors at *Forbes* interpreted it, 'dart-board investing is just as good (or just as bad) as deep-think security analysis'.[14] Based on the performance of the *Forbes* 'Dart Board Fund', it appears they may be right.

You can easily see why this would be by looking at the way the market works. It is a little bit like an election. You can 'vote' for the stock to go up by buying it, and you can 'vote' for it to go down by selling it. As in a political election, voters vote for just whatever they think will put money in their pockets. You have as many votes as you have shares of stock, and the majority rules.

Moreover, at any given time there are going to be about as many people buying your stock as there are selling it. This is why it is so easy to get in or out of the stock market. Any time you want to sell a share of stock, there is going to be someone, somewhere, who wants to buy it (unless the company is bankrupt). And any time you want to buy a stock, there is going to be someone somewhere who wants to sell it. For you to sell a share of stock there *must* be an equal and opposite buyer. Obviously, you cannot sell something if nobody wants to buy it. And that leads to our next and final point.

When you sell a share of stock, you are selling it to some other investor. And he is not a philanthropist. He is not buying your stock to do you a favour. He is buying because he thinks the price is going up instead of down. In other words, he thinks you are wrong.

Now bear in mind that this person reads the same newspapers you read, pores over the same charts as you pore over, broods over the same hot tips that you brood over, is *almost* (but perhaps not *quite*) as intelligent as you are, and he thinks you are wrong. And what makes the difference is not what the company that issues the stock is doing, but how many others there are like him out there voting against you. Remember, the majority rules.

This fact is enough in itself to explain the random walk, and it is something to think about whenever you invest in anything. No matter how sure you are that your investments are going to make money, somebody else out there thinks you are wrong. And it *has* to be this way or you could not invest in the first place.

This is why 'deep-think security analysis', as *Forbes* puts it, may be irrelevant. People do not 'vote' on the prospects of the company *behind* the stock, but on the stock itself. They bet in effect on what they think their fellow gamblers will be willing to pay for a mere piece of paper.

Professors who teach economics classes illustrate how this principle works by getting a bid started for a one pound note. The bidding may start at a couple of shillings, but as emotions rise it quickly exceeds a pound, and people have been known to bid five or six pounds for the right to possess a single pound.

If we assume that the value of a pound note is fixed, which it normally is, then this is madness. But there is no reason why one speculator should not pay two pounds for one pound if someone else out there is willing to pay him three pounds for the same pound. And why would that 'someone else' be willing to pay three pounds? Because he suspects he may find still another person who will pay four. If this makes you smile, consider the market for old coins. It is not quite as treacherous as the stock market, but that is only because the prices do not go up as fast. And we see there the very situation that I just described. People literally hoard coins and notes in the belief that others will pay *more* for them than their face value. And they are right.

Another example is the so-called gold market. I have never looked in the business section of a newspaper without seeing quarter-page ads urging people to buy gold now before its price goes through the roof. We know that a one pound note is worth one pound, yet the 'value' of gold is almost totally abstract. True, it has some uses in jewellery manufacture, and it is an excellent conductor of electricity, which makes it valuable to industry. But much of it goes into the making of Canadian Maple Leaf coins, or South African krugerrands, or bullion. And that is what determines the market. The value of gold is just whatever the next fellow is willing to pay in the belief that someone else will pay even more. Nobody knows what it is 'worth' in money terms, and nobody ever will. If someone is willing to give you a castle for a krugerrand, a krugerrand is worth a castle. If he is only willing to pour you a cup of tea for the same coin, you have made a bad investment. Anyone who watched the nonsense that took place in gold prices between 1975 and 1980 will know what I mean.

The classic example of this principle in action is the story of the South Sea Company, and I cannot leave the subject without some remarks thereon.

The South Sea Company was started by the Earl of Oxford in 1711 to trade with the King of Spain's possessions in the South Atlantic — hence the name South Sea. But the King of Spain had no interest in advancing the cause of an English company, and such trade as he was willing to permit was scarcely profitable. Nonetheless, the name of the company was kept constantly before the public, and when a bill was brought before Parliament to borrow money from the company at interest to retire the public debt, the public enthusiasm knew no bounds.

The South Sea Company was not a closely held company. Its stock was traded publicly in London's Exchange Alley, and once it looked as if it might become the public banker of sorts, the stock price started to soar. Even though Parliament had not yet decided to approve the loan, the value of a share of South Sea stock rose from 130 to 300 and beyond in a single day. Furthermore, according to Mackay, it 'continued to rise with the most astonishing rapidity during the whole time that the bill was . . . under discussion.' The directors of the company floated every kind of preposterous rumour to keep the price rising. There was to be a treaty between England and Spain, with England to get the right of free trade to all Spain's colonies. Silver was to be brought to England from the mines of Potosi-la-Paz until it was 'as common as iron'. Everyone who owned South Sea stock was to get rich. At one point the stock rose to nearly four hundred.

As the mania built up, Exchange Alley became choked with crowds, and 'Cornhill was impassible [sic] for the number of carriages. Everybody come to purchase stock. "Every fool aspired to be a knave." '[15] There simply was not enough South Sea stock to satisfy all the speculators – or peculators according to your point of view – and other schemes were offered up to meet the demand. One fellow offered shares in 'a company for carrying on an undertaking of great advantage, *but nobody to know what it is.*' And not only was nobody to know what it was, but nobody ever found out. The originator of this scheme was simple deluged with people begging him to take their money for shares – which he did. After he had pocketed £2,000 from a thousand investors in a mere five hours he left for the Continent and was never seen again.

Someone else started a company 'for the transmutation of quicksilver into a malleable fine metal', which happens to be impossible, and someone else 'for extracting silver from lead'. There was even a scheme for building 'a wheel for perpetual motion'. All these companies prospered, even though some of them were not even in business, and the South Sea Company prospered most of all.

On 28 May South Sea stock was trading for 550. After four more days of furious trading it had risen to 890. There was a brief dip in price as investor confidence sagged, and then it started up again, each day breaking the record set the day before, until the price reached as high as 1000. It seemed nobody could lose money. Immense fortunes had already been made by some of Britain's most prominent citizens, and lesser mortals invested everything they had in the expectation of making more. By this time, though, the Company's directors had figured out what the rest of us have been unable to see, despite the two hundred and sixty-four years that have passed since then. As Malkiel interprets it, they came to realize 'that the price of the shares in the market bore no relationship to the real prospects of the company,' and 'they sold out in the summer.'[16]

The price of their stock collapsed.

5

An Esoteric Look at Time

'The period of mortal life is similar from beginning to end, and
it is inevitable that according to the determined cycles the same
things always have happened, are now happening, and will
happen [in the future].'

                                                            — Origen[1]

An alterntaive to the randomness view of things is to think of
luck as a *cyclic* phenomenon. If you are having a streak of bad
luck according to this theory, then your luck cycle must be on
a negative phase. If you can figure out how long these cycles
are, and when they begin and end, you will be able to *predict*
when your luck will be good or bad. This view of things was
very popular with the ancients, and is the basis for the science
of astrology.

The most basic cycle of course is the human life cycle — the
period from birth to death. Pythagoras believed that this period
should be divided into four seasons of twenty years each which
corresponded to the seasons of the year. Spring in this system
corresponds to childhood and adolescence — the years from birth
to age twenty. Summer corresponds to adulthood — the years
from twenty-one to forty. Autumn corresponds to mature
adulthood — thus the expression 'the autumn of life'. And of
course winter corresponds to old age — the final twenty years
of life from age sixty-one to eighty.[2]

A much more popular system, though, divided the human life

cycle into *seven* periods, which were known as the seven *ages.*
Those of my readers who are at all familiar with Shakespeare
will remember this idea from *As You Like It,* where Jacques
describes the seven ages in the following famous words:

> All the world's a stage,
> And all the men and women merely players;
> They have their exits and their entrances;
> And one man in his time plays many parts,
> His acts being seven ages.

1

> At first the infant,
> Mewling and puking in the nurse's arms.

2

> Then the whining schoolboy, with his satchel,
> And shining morning face, creeping like snail
> Unwillingly to school.

3

> And then the lover,
> Sighing like furnace, with a woeful ballad
> Made to his mistress' eyebrow.

4

> Then a soldier,
> Full of strange oaths, and bearded like the pard,
> Jealous of honour, sudden and quick in quarrel,
> Seeking the bubble reputation
> Even in the cannon's mouth.

5

> And then the justice
> In fair round belly with good capon lin'd,
> With eyes severe and beard of formal cut,
> Full of wise saws and modern instances;
> And so he plays his part.

6

The sixth age shifts
Into the lean and slipper'd pantaloon,
With spectacles on his nose and pouch on side,
His youthful hose well sav'd a world too wide
For his shrunk shank; and his big manly voice,
Turning again towards childish treble, pipes
And whistles in his sound.

7

Last scene of all,
That ends this strange eventful history,
Is second childishness and mere oblivion,
Sans teeth, sans eyes, sans taste, sans everything.

Plutarch argues that the seven ages begin before one is born. The first age is from conception until birth, after which come infancy, childhood, adolescence, adulthood, mature adulthood, and old age, whereas Ptolemy, who was an astrologer, after all, relates the seven ages to the seven astrological planets then known to man.

In his *Tetrabiblos*, Ptolemy says that infancy is under the rulership of the Moon, and lasts four years, according to the Moon's 'cycle'. Its 'rapidity of growth' and 'highly variable habit' as well as 'mental incompleteness' are all characteristic in his mind of the Lunar influence.

After infancy of course comes childhood, which is under the dominance of the planet Mercury, and lasts ten years — again, according to the planet's astrological cycle. Since Mercury has to do with the intellectual side of man's nature, Ptolemy says that 'the intellectual and reasoning faculties of the mind begin to take their character' during this period of life, 'imbibing the seeds of learning, and developing, as it were, the elements and germs of the genius and abilities, and their peculiar quality. The mind is also aroused to discipline and instruction, and its first exercises.'

The third period is that of adolescence and sexual awakening, and it is obvious that this period of life must correspond to Venus. It lasts eight years, according to that planet's astrological rhythms, and leads to 'the movement of the seminal vessels . . . as well as unrestrained impetuosity and precipitancy in amours.'

The fourth period of life is that of adulthood, and corresponds in Ptolemy's opinion to the Sun, which means that it lasts nineteen years. 'Authority of action now commences in the mind,' says Ptolemy, 'the career of life is entered upon, distinction and glory are desired, and puerile irregularities are relinquished for more orderly conduct, and the pursuit of honour.'

'Mars . . . claims the fifth age,' which lasts fifteen years. 'He induces greater austerity of life, together with vexation, care, and trouble.'

The sixth age belongs to Jupiter, and lasts twelve years. It is a time for 'the relinquishment of labour, of hazardous employment and tumult, and produces greater gravity, foresight, prudence and sagacity, favouring the claim to honour, respect, and privilege.'

Finally, the seventh age, which is of course *old* age, belongs to Saturn, 'as agreeing with its chilliness. He obstructs the mental movements, the appetites and enjoyments; rendering them imbecile and dull, in conformity with the dullness of his own motion.'[3]

Hippocrates, on the other hand, says that the seven ages are *themselves* divided into sevenfold periods – and these, he says, are periods of seven years duration. He says that 'in the nature of man there are seven seasons, which men call ages: infancy, childhood, boyhood, and the rest. He is an infant till he reaches his seventh year, the age of the shedding of his teeth. He is a child till he reaches the age of puberty, which takes place in fourteen years. He is a boy till his beard begins to grow, and that time is the end of the third period of seven years. He is a youth until the completion of the growth of his whole body, which coincides with the fourth seven years. Then he is a man till he reaches his forty-ninth year, or seven times seven periods. He is a middle aged man till he is fifty-six, or eight times seven years old; and after that he is an old man.'[4]

According to Herodotus, Solon told King Croesus that the years of men were three score and ten – which is to say ten periods of *seven* years each.[5] We know that Solon supported this interpretation of the seven ages because he refers to it in a poem, which has been preserved for us by Philo of Alexandria in his treatise *On the Creation:*

> In seven years from th' earliest breath,
> The child puts forth his hedge of teeth;
> When strengthened by a similar span,

He first displays some signs of man.
As in a third his limbs increase,
A beard builds o'er his changing face.
When he has passed a fourth such time,
His strength and vigour's in its prime.
When five times seven years o'er his head
Have passed, the man should think to wed;
At forty-two, the wisdom's clear
To shun vile deeds of folly or fear:
While seven times seven years to sense
Add ready wit and eloquence.
And seven years further skill admit
To raise them to their perfect height.
When nine such periods have passed,
His powers, though milder grown, still last;
When God has granted ten times seven,
The aged man prepares for Heaven.[6]

In *The Magus*, Francis Barrett argues that there are cycles of seven months, seven days and even seven hours in man's affairs. He says, for example, that the first seven hours of an infant's life determine whether it will live or not, 'for that which will bear the breath of air after that hour, will live.' He continues:

After seven days, it casts off the relics of the navel. After twice seven days, its sight begins to move after the light. In the third seventh, it turns its eyes and whole face freely. After seven months it breeds teeth. After the second seventh month, it sits without fear of falling. After the third seventh month, it begins to speak. After the fourth seventh month, it stands strongly and walks. After the fifth seventh month, it begins to refrain sucking its nurse. After seven years, its first teeth fall, and new are bred, fitter for harder meat, and its speech is perfected. After the second seventh year, boys wax ripe and there is a beginning of generation. At the third seventh year, they grow to men in stature, and begin to be hairy, and become able and strong for generation. At the fourth seventh year they cease to grow taller. In the fifth seventh year they attain to the perfection of their strength. The sixth seventh year, they keep their strength. The seventh seventh year, they attain to their utmost discretion and wisdom, and the perfect age of men. But when they come to the tenth seventh year, where the number seven is taken for a complete number, they come to the common term of life — the prophet saying our age [which is to say our life expectancy] is seventy years.[7]

Tacitus pointed out that the Jews gave the seventh day and the seventh year to inaction, and he interprets this in the light of the fact that 'seven stars . . . rule the destinies of men' and that 'many of the heavenly bodies complete their revolutions and courses in multiples of seven.'[8] The most obvious of these is of course the Moon, which changes phase every *seven* days.

Trithemius was so impressed with the significance of the number seven in connection with cycles that he worked out an elaborate theory of history on that basis. It was published in a book called *De septem secundeis,* and proposed that the lifetime of the world could be divided into seven ages, just as can the lifetime of a single man.

Eliphas Levi described it as 'a key of all the prophecies, ancient and modern, and a mathematical means, historical and facile, of surpassing Isaiah and Jeremiah in the prevision of all the grand events of the future.'[9] Each of the seven ages of the world is assigned to one of the seven angels of the Kabbalah, and is said to last 354 years and 4 months. The first is assigned to Orifiel, 'the angel of Saturn', and begins on 13 March, because Trithemius believed that the world was created on that date. How he fixed it so precisely, he does not tell us. The successive ages are assigned to the angels of Venus, Jupiter, Mercury, Mars, the Moon, and finally the Sun, which corresponds to the seventh and last period. Michael is the angel of the Sun, and his reign, according to Trithemius, began in November 1879, in which year should have been founded 'a universal kingdom, . . . prepared by three and a half centuries of anguish and three and a half centuries of hopes.'[10] Taken literally, of course, Trithemius' prophecies seem not to have come true. But it is interesting to note that it is in this time period that many Eastern mystics believe the reign of the Maitreya was inaugurated, although his kingdom, while destined ultimately to bring peace to the inner selves of students of Buddhism, is not an earthly and visible one. It was also about this time — in 1875 — that the Theosophical Society was founded in New York, and started to promote Eastern ideas to the spiritually decadent West.

Whether you accept Trithemius' interpretation of it or not, though, it is a fact that cycles tend to be sevenfold in character, and the reason for it has to do with the nature of time.

Picture, if you will, a railway track which extends as far as you can see both before you and behind you. You are riding on this track in a small open railway carriage which allows you to see everything that is going on around you as you progress. And as the car moves forward, you can see people to your right and left living out their lives, raising their children, earning their livings, and passing forever beyond your gaze as you continue to ride further and further into the future.

If you think of the stretch of track behind you as the 'Past', and that part of the track that happens to be in front of you as the 'Future', and if you think of your little railroad car as the 'Present', you have an idea of the popular conception of Time. The three elements of Past, Present, and Future are what philosophers call the 'Three Realities' of Time, and they differ from our railroad track analogy only in that Past and Future are thought to be infinite, whereas the Present is thought to be an infinitesimal nothing separating them. If we tried to illustrate this concept diagrammatically — and we may as well — it would look something like this:

PAST--------I--------FUTURE
PRESENT

The 'Present' moves, as it were, from left to right, from the Past to the Future, and leaves behind it innumerable relics of Presents past. This 'time-track' conception of time is implicit in Minkowski's four-dimensional geometry, which was taken up with legendary success by Albert Einstein in 1905. But there are some interesting problems with it which are not at all obvious.

This fact was first pointed out by Immanuel Kant in the eighteenth century, in a book called *Critique of Pure Reason.* Try to imagine that this very afternoon Time suddenly comes to an end. You are not just out of time or short of time — there *is* no time. It stops completely. You reach the end of the railroad track.

Of course, in a sense this may happen to all of us, since we all are going to die some day. But try to imagine non-existence. You can easily imagine yourself as a corpse, but try to imagine that you do not even *exist.* It is impossible because the mere act of imagining presupposes the existence of someone to *do* the imagining.

Another way of doing this little experiment of the mind is to try to imagine that you are walking down the street and suddenly come to the end of space. We can easily imagine the universe being finite (Einstein thought it was egg-shaped). But if you imagine a finite universe, you tend to think of something being *outside* of it. That the edge of the universe could be where space actually comes to an end is rather difficult for the mind to conceive. It is difficult to imagine that there is nothing 'on the other side' of the end of space. We cannot conceive of it. We are literally forced to think of space as infinite.

Now this kind of certainty — where a thing seems so self-evident to you that you cannot conceive of it in any other way — is what philosophers call *apodeictic* certainty. It is more than just conviction; it is compulsion. You *cannot* imagine a time when there is no more time. And yet it is impossible to base this kind of certainty on any experience. Nobody has been to the end of space, after all, and nobody has ever seen time come to an end. And it is impossible to prove experimentally that time *cannot* come to an end. We just 'know' without knowing *how* we know, and yet we cannot imagine that we are wrong.

These facts led Kant to conclude that time and space are *mental*, and not *physical*, realities. They are part of the way in which our minds interpret the world around us. The notion that time and space are in any way objective seemed to him to be a mere illusion.

To that the Eastern philosopher would reply that *everything* we call 'reality' is mere illusion. In some way that we cannot comprehend intellectually, but to the understanding of which we may approach in states of deep trance, there is no final distinction between subjective and objective 'realities'. Time and space, he would say, are indeed products of the mind, but they are not for that reason to be distinguished from the things around us. For the things around us are products of the mind as well.

In any event, it is plain that our study of time should begin within, and the best place to start is with the nature of the Three Realities — Past, Present, and Future.

From the psychological point of view, it is obvious that we can only distinguish Past from Present and Present from Future because we experience them in different ways. Present is just whatever happens to be going on around us, whereas Past is what we can *remember*. Thus we derive our concept of the Present from our senses, whereas we derive our concept of Past from our memories. If we could not remember events which are clearly not part of the here-and-now, and yet which are somehow with us anyway, we would have no concept of Past at all, or Time, for that matter. Moreover, we sense a difference between Past and Present because we sense them in entirely different ways. This is what we mean when we say that Present is an objective experience, and that Past is subjective. With that in mind, it might not be unreasonable to re-draw our diagram. Instead of a straight line bisected by the Present, we therefore have a broken line, which looks something like this:

PAST   FUTURE

                                    SUBJECTIVE EXPERIENCE

        ---------------------- · ----------------------

              PRESENT   OBJECTIVE EXPERIENCE

Now there is some question about how the idea of there being a Future presents itself to us. We probably sense it by a process of elimination. In other words, the Future is *probably* just whatever is left over after we have accounted for the Present and the Past. But that is not *necessarily* true. Plutarch, who was an ancient occultist as well as historian, speculated that there might be an actual 'sense' of some kind by which we become aware of the Future, in the same way that memory is a 'sense' by which we become aware of the Past. This is how he explained prophecies. But *whatever* experiences we use, it is obvious that they are not 'objective'. And that being the case, we are safe in lumping the Future and Past in a single category as 'subjective' knowledge.

In addition to the three realities of time, there is also the sense that time 'passes', and this leads us to the next phenomenon.

We might think that time seems to 'pass' because our store of memories increases, but that is not quite true. You are much more aware of the passage of time when life is boring, yet you are more aware of acquiring memories when life is interesting. So it is obvious that a sense of time passing has to do with something other than memory, and what it *does* have to do with is sensation.

This was worked out in ancient times by Aristotle and has been confirmed since by modern psychologists. We tend to think of the Present as having no duration whatever, but it is actually a discrete interval of time. Psychologists call it the *specious* present. And instead of our consciousness of the Present being something continuous, it is in fact punctuated. As Aristotle put it, it is a series of NOWs, so that instead of the Eternal NOW, psychologically at least we have something more like NOW, NOW, NOW. As we sense that so many of thse NOWs have passed by, we sense that so much of time itself has passed.

This is why time seems to pass more quickly when you are distracted. You tend not to notice the procession of NOWs, and you are fooled as it were into thinking that there have only been a few of them. As Einstein put it, when he was standing on the street corner waiting for his girlfriend, five minutes seemed like five hours. But when he was with her, five hours seemed like five minutes. In the one case he was aware of the accumulation of NOWs, and in the other he was not.

Now, these NOWs come in discrete chunks of time because we sense things by sort of taking snapshots of the world. This is how it is possible for motion pictures to create the illusion of continuous motion by flashing a series of photographs at the audience in rapid succession. If we perceived the world by looking at it continuously, that would not work. But in fact our awareness is broken up into discrete intervals of alternating attention and inattention.

We direct our attention first toward the world, to sense what is going in on, then away from it, to appreciate what we have sensed. It is like taking a picture of something with an instant camera. You have to first direct your attention toward the scene you are photographing, then toward the picture you have taken. Consciousness works the same way. We are therefore constantly alternating our awareness between the subjective and the objective, so that instead of a broken line, time becomes a cycle, thus:

PAST   FUTURE

. . . .

.   .   SUBJECTIVE EXPERIENCE

.

.   .

--------------------------- · ----------------------------

PRESENT   OBJECTIVE EXPERIENCE

Interpreted this way, it is obvious that the conviction that we have that time is 'infinite', and which Kant referred to, comes from the fact that a cycle has no beginning and no end.

The only way time itself can 'end' is therefore, as I said earlier, for one to die. In that event (and that assumes that there is no immortality, in which I happen to believe), the cycle stops and all the three realities disappear with the final extinction of consciousness.

Now, thus far we have left things at the simple division between subjective and objective, but there are four categories of conscious experience according to Analytical Psychology, and that means the 'subjective' area of our diagram has to be divided into three parts. The four categories are thoughts, feelings, sensations, and intuitions, and of these only sensations can be considered objective.

If we include thoughts, feelings, and intuitions on our diagram, it looks something like this:

PAST   FUTURE

1 7   PSYCHIC CONSCIOUSNESS

.   .

2 6   MENTAL CONSCIOUSNESS

.   .

3 . . . 5   EMOTIONAL CONSCIOUSNESS

.   .

4   SENSE CONSCIOUSNESS

PRESENT

So here we have not only a cycle, but a cycle of *seven steps*. If the psychological process whereby we acquire a consciousness of time is sevenfold in nature, it should not be surprising that our consciousness of time itself should also be sevenfold. The ancients believed this to be the reason we tend to think of cycles of time as properly divided into seven periods, and they also held that this sevenfold cycle exists in the objective world as well as in the subjective.

If this is true, then it follows that there are precisely *four* different types of conscious experiences and not three or six because there are precisely four different types of realities in the world to consciously experience. An experience of thought is qualitatively different from an experience of feeling. And an experience of feeling is qualitatively different from an experience of sensation. We distinguish these from each other because we experience them differently, just as we distinguish Past from Present because we experience them differently.

Now sensation is consciousness of matter, and most people accept the fact that matter is not something which merely exists in consciousness. It is an objective reality which is found in nature. We do not afford that same status to the objects of our emotional consciousness, however, or our mental or intuitive consciousness. We assume that, when we become conscious of feelings, we are aware of something which exists only within ourselves. However, there is no way to prove that this is true, and if it *is* true, we are led into insolvable philosophical difficulties.

For that reason, esoteric philosophy maintains that feelings are experiences of a universal reality in nature which happens not to be material, and which has nothing to do with the material plane, but which is real, nonetheless. Likewise, thoughts are not truly subjective experiences in the sense that we usually think of them as subjective. They, too, are experiences of a universal reality in nature which is non-material but which is nevertheless real, and which is also non-emotional.

We refer to these things as *meta*-physical realities to distinguish them from physical realities, and to distinguish them from each other we sometimes refer them to different 'planes' of existence. Thus in addition to the physical 'plane', we find writers such as Dion Fortune making reference to the emotional 'plane', the mental 'plane', and the spiritual 'plane'. In the Kabbalah they are referred to as the Four Worlds.

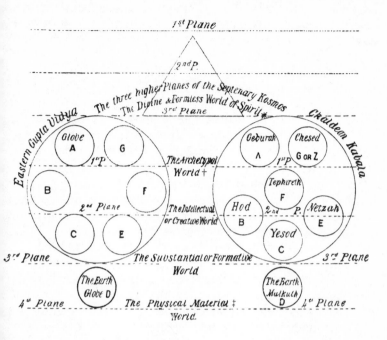

Kabbalistic and Eastern ideas contrasted. From H.P. Blavatsky, *The Secret Doctrine*, 1888 edition.

This is self-evident on close inspection, because consciousness does not exist just in man but throughout nature. Anything which responds to its environment, in however rudimentary a manner, can be said to have 'consciousness' of sorts, because that is all that consciousness really is. And anything of which we can be conscious necessarily 'responds' to its environment, otherwise there would be nothing for us to be conscious of.

You may never have thought of it this way, but if you hold this book between your fingers, and try to press your fingers together, the material of which the book is made resists the pressure, and this resistance constitutes a rudimentary 'response' to the environment, which in this case is the pressure being exerted by your finger. If it did not 'respond' by offering resistance to your fingers, you would be able to bring both your fingers together, and you would have no sensation of them passing through anything. So far as your sense of touch was concerned, the book would cease to exist.

Likewise, if light waves are directed toward the book's jacket, some of those light waves are reflected. This reflection is caused by the jacket itself, and this fact of causing light waves to reflect from its surface constitutes a rudimentary 'response' to the environment. If this 'response' did not occur, the book would cease to exist so far as your sense of sight is concerned. It would become invisible.

Now I am not going to suggest that the 'consciousness' which is displayed by a piece of inanimate matter is as highly organized or as interesting as the consciousness which is found in man. But it is consciousness, nonetheless. The ability to respond to the environment is consciousness in its most primitive form, and anything that we can sense responds to its environment.

That is why we say that there is consciousness in man because there is consciousness in nature, and because man is part of nature. It is also why we say that there are four different types of conscious experiences in man because there are four different types of conscious experiences in nature. Man merely displays in himself the divisions of nature itself, and that leads to our next point.

In *The Secret Doctrine*, Madame Blavatsky argues that the consciousness-cycle in man – the cycle of seven steps – is also found in nature. Thus, anything which displays the existence of consciousness (which is *anything*, as I have said) must be going through the alternating cycles of introversion and extroversion of consciousness, just as is man. This leads us to two interesting conclusions: first, that this cycle manifests in nature as the universal law of vibration, and second, that these cycles govern the appearance and eventual dissolution of all things.

In Madame Blavatsky's interpretation, that aspect of the cycle in which awareness turns from the plane of intuitive experience to the plane of sensations is known as the 'Descent Into Matter'. It is symbolized in Jewish mythology by the 'Fall of Man', the 'Garden of Eden' allegorically representing the world of Spirit, or the 'plane' of intuitional or psychic experiences, and man's habitation after the 'Fall' representing the world of sensations. This phase of the cycle is also referred to as *involution*.

The reverse aspect of the cycle, in which attention turns away from sensation and toward so-called 'subjective' experiences is the 'Ascent to Spirit', or the *evolutionary* phase. Since there are four 'involutionary' and three 'evolutionary' steps, to make a total

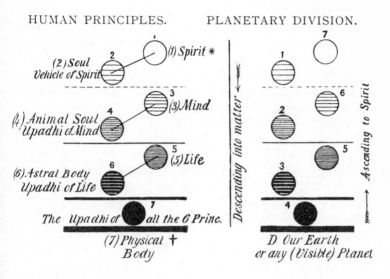

The seven Theosophical principles — from Madame Blavatsky, *The Secret Doctrine*, 1888 edition.

of seven, we say that four is the number of the body, and three the number of the soul.

Interpreting this in terms of the human life cycle, we can see that the first period of seven years should be one of psychic development, which it apparently is. Psychic ability tends to be more active in most of us during early childhood than during any other period of life, and children take a keen interest in stories which suggest that there may be possibilities in nature undreamt of by their more materialistically-oriented elders. Madame

Blavatsky says that the *Atma* in man awakens at the end of the first seven year period.[11]

The second period would then be a period of intellectual development, beginning at the age of seven, which is traditionally the Age of Reason. In recognition of this fact, school systems thoughout the world educate children during the seven years between seven and fourteen, although in some places the process may begin at a slightly earlier age, and continue beyond the end of the period.

The third period would then be a period of emotional development, and this certainly would be an apt description of adolescence. It is at age fourteen that puberty begins, and it is in the seven years thereafter that the secondary sex characteristics begin to mature and that individuals are prepared for their respective reproductive roles.

Madame Blavatsky maintains that in this at least the individual relives the history of the race. There is little real difference between boys and girls during the first two seven year periods of life, and, for that reason, Blavatsky surmises that man himself was bisexual or androgynous during the first two Root Races, combining the functions of both sexes in a single body. Then, just as sexual differentiation begins in the individual during the third seven year period, so man as a species began to evolve into two definite sexes during the third Root Race, which inhabited the continent of Lemuria.

The fourth period starts at age twenty-one, which has been recognized legally as the age of legal competence. During this period the individual's physical development is completed, and according to Blavatsky's theories we would expect him to reach the peak of his physical prowess halfway through the fourth seven year cycle, or at about age twenty-five. This is exactly what science says happens, and this peak is followed by a decline in physical strength, just as the esoteric principles would predict. In the evolution of the human race, the fourth period of human life corresponds to the fourth Root Race, which lived on the continent of Atlantis, and we find that the Atlanteans are supposed to have been endowed with exceptional physical strength. Man has been declining physically since the fourth race, just as the individual declines physically after the fourth seven year period.

If we take Madame Blavatsky's principles one step further, we can see that there are shorter cycles nested within the seven year periods – thus we have cycles of seven months, seven days, seven hours and some say even seven minutes. Some of these shorter cycles can have some value to us, and there are ways of determining when they begin and end – brought to us as usual by the yogis of the Far East.

6
Some Yogic Methods

'To everything there is a season, and a time to every purpose under the sun: A time to be born, and a time to die; a time to plant, and a time to pluck up that which is planted.'

— *Ecclesiastes*

The cyclic nature of time and the sevenfold nature of cycles can be seen in astrological influences as well as in the more occult principles emphasized by Esoteric Buddhism. Time is measured by planetary motions, after all, and there are seven astrological planets, whose rotations describe cycles. This is no coincidence, as we shall see. It could almost be said that the planets show exoterically what we see esoterically in the nature of consciousness itself.

We have already seen that in his *Tetrabiblos* Ptolemy referred the seven 'ages' of man to the seven astrological planets. In her 'Secret Instructions' to members of the Esoteric Section of the Theosophical Society, Madame Blavatsky speculated that the correspondence which exists between the planetary influences and the 'principles' of Esoteric Buddhism was the real basis for the original science of astrology, although she describes the astrology known today as an 'exoteric', rather than an 'esoteric', science. I suspect that this is true, and I think it would be worthwhile, therefore, to take a look at some of the esoteric theories behind astrology. Astrologers have been criticized more than once for putting too much emphasis on *practice* at the expense of *theory*, but theory there certainly is, and one of the most eminent theorists this field has ever had is Paracelsus.

'To obtain a correct idea of the construction of the Microcosm,' he says, 'we should know how the Macrocosm is constructed; we must look upon man as an integral part of universal nature, and not as something separate or different from [it].'[1] 'Mars, Venus, or Jupiter in the sky' are produced, according to Paracelsus, by an 'element' which 'exists also in the body of man, because the [astral body of man] is the son of the astral body of the Macrocosm in the same sense as the physical body of man is the son of the earth.'[2] This astral or 'invisible man is hidden in the visible one, and is formed in the shape of the outer one as long as it remains in that outer one.' It is, so to speak, 'the shadow or the counterpart of the material body. As man's picture is reflected in a mirror, so the form of the physical man is reflected in the invisible body.'[3]

Now 'the action of the stars upon the invisible body of man may be explained' by the fact that this 'invisible body is made up of the same elements as the stars', and can in a sense be considered 'an emanation of the latter.'[4] 'It contains the elements of all cosmic influences,' says Paracelsus, and its 'essences' are 'intimately related to the sidereal essences of the stars.'[5]

Paracelsus explains that the astral body is literally 'nourished by the Astral Light' just as the physical body is nourished by the elements of the earth. And 'as the [physical body of man] hungers and thirsts for the elements of the earth, so the [astral body] longs [and hungers] for the influences which come from the Astral Plane.'[6]

'The Sun and the stars attract something from us, and we attract something from them, because our astral bodies are in sympathy with the stars, and the stars are in sympathy with our astral bodies.'[7] However, 'it must not be supposed that a certain material element coming from the planets enters the organism of man and adds something to it which it does not already possess. The light of the Sun does not contribute any corporeal substance to the organisms existing upon the earth, and a man does not become heavier if he stands in the sun.'[8] But nevertheless, 'the essence of man's sidereal body, which he attracts from the stars, is of a substantial nature. We consider it as being something spiritual on account of the ethereality of its substance, and on account of the great dimensions of its invisible body.'[9] 'It is ethereal in nature; still it is substance.'[10]

Now 'the influences of the Astral Light enter into the body of man as the sunshine penetrates through a glass window into a room. And as the rain is absorbed by the soil, while rocks and stones are impenetrable to it, so there are certain elements in man's organization which absorb these influences, while other elements resist their action.[11] What this means, although it is said in a very subtle manner, is that specific astral and planetary influences are absorbed by, and become centred in, specific areas of the body. In fact, Paracelsus says that 'every organ in the human body is formed by the action of certain principles that exist in the universe, and the former attract the corresponding activity in the latter.'[12] 'Thus the heart is in sympathy with the elements of the Sun, the brain with the Moon, the gall-bladder with Mars, the kidneys with Venus, the lungs with Mercury, the liver with Jupiter,[and] the spleen with Saturn.'[13] 'These organs are only the material and bodily representatives of invisible energies that pervade and circulate in the whole system; so that, for instance, the real liver is a force that circulates in all parts of the body, and has its head in that organ which we call the liver.'[14]

'The star-gazer knows only the external visible heaven; but the true astronomer knows two heavens, the external, visible, and the internal, invisible, one.'[15] 'There is a heaven and earth in man as there is in the Macrocosm, and in that heaven there are all the celestial influences, whose visible representations we see in the sky, such as the planets and stars, the Milky Way, the Zodiac et cetera, neither more nor less; for the Microcosm is an exact counterpart of the Macrocosm in every respect except its external form.'[16] He says that 'there is not a single invisible power in heaven which does not find its corresponding principle in the inner heaven of man,' and he adds that '*the above acts upon the below, and the latter reacts upon the former.*'[17]

It is worth mentioning here that this is a veiled reference to the *Emerald Tablet of Hermes*, and that what we have here is probably the only clear explanation in alchemical literature of the principles discussed in that work. According to Madame Blavatsky, 'tradition declares that [the *Emerald Tablet* was found] on the dead body of Hermes [Trismegistus] at Hebron . . . by an Isarim, an initiate. It contains in a few sentences the essence of the Hermetic wisdom,' and it contains in the first few sentences the principles we have been discussing.[18] They were brilliantly translated by the French artist Sar Peladan in his *Fils des etoiles*, thus:

> That which is above is like that which is below
> And that which is below is like that which is above.
> To accomplish the miracles of Will,
> Will rises from the Earth to the Sky,
> And then descends once more onto the Earth,
> Receiving the strength of superior and inferior things.[19]

'What is Mars,' Paracelsus asks, 'but the principle of Iron, which is found universally distributed in nature and in the constitution of man? What is Venus, but the power which excites the *Vasa spermatica* in men and animals?'[20] 'The natural forces acting in the various organs are intimately related to similar forces acting in the organism of the world, and as the liver, the spleen, the heart, et cetera, are the bodily representatives of certain activities, likewise the Sun and Moon, Venus, Mars, et cetera, are the visible representatives of the corresponding organs of the Cosmos. If a man gets angry, it is not because he has too much bile, but because the "Mars", the combative element in his body (the invisible power that guides the production of bile), is in a state of exaltation. If a man is amorous, it is not because his spermatic vessels are overloaded, but because the "Venus" (the amorous element) in his body is in a state of exaltation. If in such cases a conjunction of the combative and amorous elements takes place in his body, an ebullition of jealousy may be the cause; and if such an internal conjunction should take place at a time when conjunctions of the planets Mars and Venus takes place in the sky, the sympathetic relationship existing between the elements representing these planets in the Microcosm with elements represented by those of the Macrocosm may lead to serious consequences unless counteracted by the superior power of reason and will.'[21] Paracelsus insisted that Hippocrates was right when he said that 'the wise man rules the stars.' 'As the wisdom of the Supreme guides the motions of the stars,' Paracelsus thought, 'so the reason of man rules the influences which rotate and circulate in his soul.' As the astrologers say, the stars *im*-pel and do not *com*-pel.

Now let us start with the two most important planets: the Sun and the Moon. The Sun in the sky corresponds to a 'Sun' in man, according to Paracelsus, and likewise the Moon in the sky corresponds to a 'Moon' in man. Furthermore, 'the seat of the Sun in the Microcosm is in the heart [and] that of the Moon is in the brain.'[22]

This is intended in more than just a metaphorical sense, because Paracelsus says that not only do the Sun in the sky and the 'Sun' in man *correspond* with each other, but they function in a similar manner as well. Many years before William Harvey was born, Paracelsus wrote that 'the human blood contains an airy, fiery spirit, and this spirit has its centre in the heart, where it is most condensed, *and from which it radiates, and the radiating rays return to the heart.* Likewise, the world has its fiery spirit pervading the atmosphere, and its centre is called the Sun, and the influences radiating from the Sun return to that centre.'[23] This is obviously a veiled reference to the circulation of the blood, and in another place Paracelsus says that 'all the members of the body are potentially contained in the vital fluid, which has its seat in the brain, *while the activity which propels it comes from the heart.*'[24]

Madame Blavatsky said pretty much the same thing in *The Secret Doctrine.* 'There is a regular circulation of the vital fluid throughout our [solar] system,' she wrote, 'of which the Sun is the heart. [This process is] the same as the circulation of the blood in the human body, the Sun contracting as rhythmically as the human heart does, only instead of performing the round in a second or so, it takes the solar "blood" ten of its years [to circulate] and a whole year to pass through its auricles and ventricles and thence to the great veins and arteries of the system.' This gives us 'the fixed cycle of eleven years when the number of solar spots increases, which is due to the contraction of the solar heart.'[25] Theosophists have a number of interesting ideas about the Sun, and some of those have since been corroborated by Science. In the *Mahatma Letters* the Mahatma K.H. suggested that the Sun was 'full of iron vapours' and 'electric and magnetic matter in its sixth and seventh state.' [*sic*][26] This was a scientific heresy when it was written, but some forty years later scientists found that it was true. The Sun is indeed full of 'iron vapours'. Moreover, the extraordinary heat which these iron atoms must withstand strips the outermost twenty-six electrons from them, leaving them in a 'state' that cannot be found naturally anywhere on earth. If we permit ourselves to interpret the Mahatma's reference to the 'sixth and seventh states' as meaning states unlike the four states known to science, it would seem that this bit of Theosophical teaching has been confirmed.

Now with that said, it should also be pointed out that the heart and the brain are traditional locations of certain *chakras*, or centres of psychic power in the human body. The heart is the location of the Anahat Chakra, and the brain is the location of two chakras — the Ajna and the Sahasrara. The Ajna chakra is located between the eyebrows, and corresponds to the Third Eye, or pineal gland, and the Sahasrara is located at the top of the head. Moreover, the heart and the brain were considered in ancient times the two seats of man's understanding.

This gets us into a heresy, I am afraid, because modern man does not 'think' with his heart, unless he is a poet. But even scientists recognize that there are two aspects, or two polarities if you will, to man's understanding, and in the more modern view these are assigned not to the head and heart but to the two hemispheres of the brain.

The left side of the brain is supposed to be masculine, rational, logical, and a lover of science and mathematics, whereas the right side of the brain is supposed to be feminine, artistic, poetic, creative, and irrational. Madame Blavatsky has this same idea in her 'Secret Instructions'. 'Man is androgyne, so far as his head is concerned', she says, and she attributes one polarity to the pineal, and the other to the pituitary gland.[27] This happens to be consistent with the Eastern view of things, because yogis attribute the influence of the Sun and Moon not to the heart and brain but to the Ajna and Sahasrara chakras. The heart centre in yoga is said to be the seat of the influence of one of the lesser planets. But this is the only principle on which the alchemists and yogis disagree. Everywhere else, they seem to be as one.

Now the right side of the brain dominates the left side of the body, and the left side of the brain dominates the right side of the body, so we see that this essential polarity in man has to do with more than just what goes on inside your head. This would hardly be news to the yogis, who have taught this very thing for thousands of years. They have always maintained that the right side of the body is positive in polarity, and that it corresponds to the influence of the Sun. The left side of the body is therefore negative in polarity and corresponds to the influence of the Moon. And these are actual physical polarities, which distinguish the kinds of energies in the two sides of the body.

This was demonstrated in England at the turn of the century by Dr Walter John Kilner, who showed that by bringing the finger tips of the right and left hands together, the human aura could be intensified and made easier to see.

If the right and left sides of the body manifest two different polarities, the yogis maintain that this should also be true of the organs located on those two sides, and that should extend to the two lungs, one of which is located on the right side of the body, and one of which is located on the left. Since the right side of the body manifests the so-called Sun, or positive, polarity, and since the right lung is part of the right side of the body, the yogis maintain that the right lung should be associated with the Sun polarity as well. They furthermore insist that the breath which is associated with the right lung should be considered the Sun Breath, in consideration of this fact of polarity, and this Sun Breath of course enters and leaves the body through the right nostril.

The left lung and the left nostril are therefore associated with the Moon polarity, or the negative polarity, which manifests throughout the left side of the body, and that means that the breath which enters and leaves through the left nostril is in yoga called the Moon Breath. This is the origin of the word 'Hatha', as in *Hatha Yoga*. 'Ha-tha' means literally 'Sun-Moon', and the yogis instruct us that the Sun and Moon breaths are literally to be understood as having to do with the Sun and Moon in the sky, as I have explained.

Now these facts are used throughout yoga, in breathing exercises, in developing the postures called *asanas*, and also in certain exercises called *mudras* in which the fingers are brought together in certain ways. All of these things are done to bring the Sun and Moon polarities in the human body together in particular ways, and to produce certain yogically interesting results.

They are also useful for divination, and this is where we connect with luck.

At a given moment, if the Sun happens to be the more dominant planet in its influence upon your astral body, that means the energy associated with the Sun polarity will manifest itself more strongly than the energy which is associated with the Moon polarity. And *that* shows up in your breathing.

When the energy associated with the Sun polarity is more active in your astral body, those organs which are located on the right side of your body will be more active than those located on the left side of your body. So say the yogis, anyway. And those organs include your right lung. Hence, you know if the Sun is dominant over the Moon at any given time because you will breathe more heavily through your right nostril than through your left. Likewise, when the Moon polarity is dominant, you will breathe more heavily through your left nostril than through your right.

It is very easy for you to test this principle, even if you are not a yogi. Simply place your fingertips under your nostrils and breathe normally. If you feel your breath more vigorously coming out of your right nostril, then you will know that the Sun Breath is dominant. If you feel your breath coming more vigorously out of your left nostril, then you will know that the Moon Breath is dominant. And if it appears to be coming out of each nostril with about equal force, you will know that you are in what yogis call the 'Susumna Breath'. 'Susumna' is the esoteric name for the spinal cord, and this Susumna Breath is said to be particularly favourable for the study and practice of yoga.

If the Sun or the Moon Breaths are dominant, this indicates that conditions are favourable or unfavourable for certain kinds of activities. An early explorer in Northern India wrote that the yogis could 'tell future events by the breath of their nostrils, according as the right or left orifice is more or less open,' and he adds that 'those only can believe all this who have seen it with their own eyes.'[28]

The Key of Solomon recommends the days which are ruled by the Moon for embassies, voyages, envoys, messages, navigation, reconciliation, love, and the acquisition of merchandise by water.' The hours of the Moon are 'proper for making experiments relating to recovery of stolen property, for obtaining nocturnal visions, for summoning spirits in sleep, and for preparing anything relating to water.'[29]

Paracelsus says 'the power represented by [the Moon] rules agriculture, nautical affairs, [and] travels,' and it is known to be favourable to all these general kinds of activities. It has a negative side as well though. According to Paracelsus the influence of the Moon is 'cold', whereas the Sun's influence is warm, and the Lunar influence 'acts upon the brain and stimulates the sexual passions and causes injurious dreams and hallucinations.' This is why insane people are sometimes called 'lunatics'. According to Madame Blavatsky, 'spiritual clairvoyance is derived from the Sun' whereas 'all psychic states, disease, and even lunacy, proceed from the Moon.'[30] Esoterically, the Moon corresponds to the Astral Plane.

Aristotle, who may have made contact with yoga theories indirectly through his pupil, Alexander the Great, claimed the Moon was 'the star of the breath' just as do the Hindus because 'no animal dies except when the Moon is ebbing.' Pliny says that 'this has been widely noticed in the Gallic ocean, and has been found to hold good at all events in the case of man.'[31]

In Aristotle's view, the Moon 'saturates the earth and fills bodies by its approach, and empties them by its departure.' He believed that it was for this reason that 'shells increase in size as the Moon waxes,' and he believed that even 'the blood of human beings increases and diminishes with its light; and that also leaves and herbs are sensitive to it, the same force penetrating into all things.'[32]

When the Sun Breath is dominant, we find all the opposite influences from what we would expect from the Moon. Thus, according to Rama Prasad, the Moon Breath favours things which are to be 'durable' whereas the Sun Breath favours anything 'transitory and temporary.' Whereas the Moon Breath favours 'calm acts' the Sun Breath favours 'harsh acts'. Whereas the Moon Breath favours pursuits which are relatively more feminine in character, the Sun Breath favours activities which are relatively more masculine.

Paracelsus says that 'the power which is represented by [the Sun] rules the affairs of kings, kingly powers, and majesty; all the glory, riches, treasures, ornaments, and vanities of this world.' *The Key of Solomon* says the days dominated by the Sun are 'very good for perfecting experiments regarding temporal wealth, hope, gain, fortune, divination, the favour of princes, to dissolve hostile feeling, and to make friends.' The *hours* of the Sun 'are adapted for preparing any operations whatsoever of love, of kindness, and of *invisibility*' and 'for all extraordinary, uncommon, and unknown operations.'

Nowadays there are few princes left in the world and most people do not have occasion to deal with 'the affairs of kings, kingly powers, and majesty.' But we could infer from these descriptions that the Solar influence is excellent for dealing with persons in high places, for promoting yourself, and for activities which call for diplomacy and tact. It would also be an excellent time for any kind of speculation, for forecasting, for divination, and for making money and acquiring wealth. If opportunities like this come along, and you find that the Sun Breath is dominant at that particular moment, you may be assured that the planetary influences will be favourable to swift action. Since the Solar influence is specifically a positive influence and recommended for 'operations . . . of love [and] of kindness' we would expect that it would be an unfavourable time for dealing with enemies, except for reconciliation.

Esoterically, Madame Blavatsky says the Sun 'is the external manifestation of the seventh principle of our planetary system, while the Moon is its fourth principle, shining in the borrowed robes of her master, saturated with and reflecting every passionate impulse and evil desire of her grossly material body, Earth.'[33]

If a man and woman conceive a child and they are both breathing through the left nostril at the moment of conception, yogis say the child will be a girl. If they are both breathing through the right nostril, the child will be a boy. And if one is breathing through the left nostril and the other through the right, the child may be of either sex.

Yoga texts are full of lore like this. In a normal and healthy person the breath should change from one nostril to the other about every two hours. If the breath remains in your dominant nostril for more than two hours, you may be about to become ill. If it remains in the same nostril for a day, illness is certain. And if it remains there for a week, the illness will be serious. If the illness is caused by the Sun Breath, it will be accompanied by a fever, and if it is caused by the Moon Breath, it will be accompanied by chills.

According to the *Sivagama*, since the Moon Breath is related quite literally to the Moon in the sky, it is also affected by the Lunar Month, which has two polarities. During the two weeks that the Moon in the sky is waxing, this ancient text maintains that the Moon in man is waxing as well. Similarly, during the two weeks that the Moon in the sky is waning, the Moon in man is waning, and the relative dominance of Sun and Moon polarities in man falls to the Sun by default.

It is only necessary to use your fingertips to figure out which of these polarities is dominant, though, and with practice, it is easy to sense the dominant polarity without using your fingers. After all, you do not want to be seen publicly with your fingers up your nose, even if you *are* a yogi!

7

Some Tattwic Refinements

> 'There is a tide in the affairs of men,
> Which, taken at the flood, leads on to fortune;
> Omitted, all the voyages of their life
> Is bound in shallows and in miseries.'
> — William Shakespeare, *Julius Caesar*

The planetary influences that we discussed in the last chapter are believed by astrologers to be the result of some kind of planetary vibration. Pythagoras compared the system of the planets to the strings of a lyre. The gravitational tension that exists between the planets was, in his mind, similar to the tension on a string, and that, he believed, would naturally cause some kind of tone or sound to result. This harmony he referred to variously as the 'Music of the Spheres', the *Diapason*, or the 'Universal Harmony'.

Pythagoras is said actually to have been able to hear the Music of the Spheres, on account of his spiritual development, whereas ordinary mortals are deaf to these celestial strains. As Shakespeare has it:

> There's not the smallest orb which thou behold'st
> But in his motion like an angel sings . . .
> Such harmony is in immortal souls;
> But, whilst this muddy vesture of decay
> Doth grossly close it in, we cannot hear it.

For this 'Harmony of the Spheres' to be a *harmony* instead of a *cacophony*, it would be necessary for the 'tones' which they produce to harmonize with each other according to musical principles, and that puts some constraints on the distances that may exist between the planets. In other words, the planetary orbits cannot be arbitrary, but must be fixed by musical laws, if Pythagoras is right. According to Pliny the Elder, Pythagoras designated the distance between the Earth and the Moon as one whole tone. The distance between the Moon and Mercury he thought was a semitone, between Mercury and Venus another semitone, between Venus and the Sun a tone and a half, between the Sun and Mars a tone, between Mars and Jupiter half a tone, between Jupiter and Saturn another half tone, and between Saturn and the Zodiac a tone and a half. Saturn in this scheme of things moves in what Pythagoras called the 'Dorian' mode. Jupiter moves in the 'Phrygian' mode, and so forth, through all the seven planets, a 'refinement', which Pliny considered 'more entertaining than convincing.'[1]

It was convincing to the Egyptian astronomer Ptolemy, though, and he wrote an entire book on it, called *The Harmonies of the World*.[2] Johannes Kepler, who should have known something about matters astronomical, penned a similar volume with the same name centuries later to bring Ptolemy's speculations into line with the Copernican theory.[3] The fact that these eminent astronomers could take the Harmony of the Spheres seriously gave the theory some considerable credibility in the minds of lesser mortals, but the real shocker came when it was discovered that the distances between the planets really *do* follow a pattern similar to the one Pythagoras predicted.

An astronomer named Bode discovered this, and the principle is known as *Bode's Law* in his honour. He assigned numbers to each of the planets, starting with zero for Mercury, three for Venus, six for Earth, twelve for Mars, and so on. Then he added four to each number and divided by ten. The resulting numbers are interpreted as the distances of each of the planets from the Sun in *Astronomical Units*, one Astronomical Unit being the distance between the Sun and the Earth.

Using Bode's methods, we come up with the following theoretical distances, which I have listed together with the actual distances for comparison purposes:

Planet	Theoretical Distance	Measured Distance
Mercury	.4	.39
Venus	.7	.72
Earth	1.0	1.0
Mars	1.6	1.52
Ceres	2.8	2.65
Jupiter	5.2	5.2
Neptune	39.8	30.1
Pluto	77.2	39.5

When Bode's Law was first published in 1772, only the seven traditional astrological planets were known, and they did not include any 'planet' between Mars and Jupiter. Hence, in the year 1800, six German astronomers searched for the missing 'planet' and discovered the asteroid Ceres, whose orbit fits the prediction of the law precisely. Later, Ceres was discovered to be merely the largest of several hundreds, perhaps even thousands, of asteroids, which are assumed to be what remains of an exploded planet which once revolved 2.8 Astronomical Units from the Sun.[4]

Arnold of Villanova says that the planetary vibrations propagate through the *spiritus*, an invisible substance which is said in alchemy to permeate all space. Spiritus is to matter what the spirit is to man — hence the name — and it is said in alchemy to be the First Matter, the primordial substance from which all other substances are derived.[5]

In Arnold's view, the planetary vibrations propagate through this ocean of spiritus just as sound waves propagate through the air. We may not 'hear' them, as Pythagoras seems to suggest that we should, but they affect us, nonetheless.

This idea is by no means absurd, because everything that we can sense is either vibratory in nature or emits energies which *are* vibratory, and we must sense the planetary influences, else they would not affect us.[6] We do not hear a symphony orchestra, but rather the sound vibrations produced by their instruments. We do not see objects, but rather the light vibrations which they reflect. In fact, according to the so-called 'infrared' theory, we do not even *smell* things. Rather, we 'smell' certain vibrations which are emitted by foods and other substances, and which have wavelengths slightly longer than visible light.

Hartmann goes even further. In his *Paracelsus* he refers us to 'recent researches in chemistry, and comparisons made between the chemical, musical, and colour scales,' which 'seem to indicate that [things are not different because of] an essential difference of the substances of which they are composed, but only [because of] a difference in the number of their atomic vibrations.'[7]

Now this leads to an interesting point which has been sensed psychically by advanced students, but which is only imperfectly understood intellectually. It appears that things which are similar in some manner in the nature of their characteristic vibrations have an affinity for each other. This is known as *the principle of sympathies*, or sometimes as *the law of correspondences*, and was first pointed out by Hippocrates. The 'correspondences' or 'sympathies' that are supposed to exist between different kinds of things are often expressed in tabular form. The following is a typical table from *The Key of Solomon*:

TABLE OF CORRESPONDENCES

Day	Planet	Colour	Metal	Archangel	Angel
Sunday	Sun	Yellow	Gold	Michael	Raphael
Monday	Moon	White	Silver	Gabriel	Gabriel
Tuesday	Mars	Red	Iron	Khamael	Zamael
Wednesday	Mercury	Purple	Mercury	Raphael	Michael
Thursday	Jupiter	Blue	Tin	Tzadqiel	Sachiel
Friday	Venus	Green	Copper	Haniel	Anael
Saturday	Saturn	Black	Lead	Tzaphqiel	Cassiel

Now these 'tables of correspondences' are not based on mere superstition or folk belief. Rightly or wrongly, psychically gifted persons have maintained that there really *is* a correspondence between the Sun and Gold, for example, or between Sunday and the colour yellow. In *The Masters and the Path*, C.W. Leadbeater says that certain psychics he knew 'saw' the seven days of the week in terms of the seven colours, although he never had the experience himself.[8] The other correspondences in this table were derived in a similar manner, as we shall soon see.

Paracelsus even maintained that the colours, metals, planets and so forth were just different manifestations of the same thing. 'What is "Venus",' he asks, 'but the "Artemisia" that grows in your garden? What is "iron" but Mars? Venus and Artemisia are both the products of the same essence, and Mars and iron are both the manifestations of the same cause. He who knows what iron is, knows the attributes of Mars. He who knows Mars, knows iron.'[9]

'On this truth is based the power of amulets and talismans, and the influences which they may exercise upon the astral form of the bearer. Talismans are like boxes, in which sidereal influences may be preserved.'[10] Not only are 'our astral bodies in sympathy with the stars, and the stars in sympathy with our astral bodies' in his opinion, '*but the same is the case with the astral bodies of all other objects.* They all attract astral influences from the stars. Each body attracts certain particular influences from them; some attract more and others less.'[11] The seven alchemical metals just 'attract' the planetary influences to an unusual degree.

Hartmann interprets this to mean that 'certain substances' have 'the power . . . to absorb and to retain certain planetary influences' and that it is this power which 'is used for the purpose of investing them with occult qualities. Pure metals may be used by the alchemist for that purpose, and in this way amulets, "magic mirrors", and other things that may produce magic effects are prepared.'[12]

Especially if we bring the 'astra' of several different metals together we can, says Paracelsus,

> . . . produce wonderful effects. If we make a composition of seven metals in the proper order and at the proper time, we will obtain a metal which contains all the virtues of the seven. Such a composition is called 'electrum'. It possesses the virtues of the seven metals that enter into its composition, and the electrum is one of the most valuable preparations known to secret science. The ordinary metals cannot be compared with it on account of its magic power. A vessel made of the electrum will immediately indicate it, if any poisonous substance has been put in it, because it will begin to sweat on its outside.
>
> Many wonderful things can be made of this electrum, such as amulets, charms, magic finger-rings, arm-rings, seals, figures, mirrors, bells, medals, and many other things possessing great magic powers of which very little is publicly known, because our art has been neglected, and the majority of men do not even know that it exists.
>
> It would not be proper to explain all the virtues and powers of the electrum, because the sophist would begin to blaspheme, and

the ignorant would become angry; the idiot would ridicule, and the wicked misuse it; and we are therefore forced to be silent in regard to some of its principal virtues. But there are a few wonderful qualities which it possesses, and of which we will speak. We have observed them personally, and we know that we are speaking the truth. We have seen finger-rings made of the electrum that cured their wearers of spasms and paralytic afflictions, of epilepsy and apoplexy; and the application of such a ring, even during the most violent paroxysm of an epileptic attack, was always followed by immediate relief.* We have seen such a ring begin to sweat at the beginning of a hidden disease.

The electrum is antipathic to all evil influences, because there is hidden in it a heavenly power and the influence of all the seven planets. Therefore the Egyptians and Chaldeans and the Magi of Persia used it against evil spirits, and made great discoveries by its use. If I were to tell all I know about the virtues of the electrum, the sophists would denounce me for being the greatest sorcerer in the world.

I will, however, say that I have known a person in Spain, who possessed a bell made out of the electrum, weighing about two pounds, and by ringing that bell he could cause various kinds of spectres and apparitions to appear, and they would obey his commands. Before using the bell he always wrote some words or characters on its inside. He then rang the bell, and immediately the spirits appeared in such a shape as he ordered them to take. He was even able to attract by the sound of that bell the spectres of men or animals, or to drive them away when they were not wanted; and whenever he wanted another spirit to appear he wrote some other characters on the inside of that bell. He refused to tell me the secret of these words and characters, but I meditated about it, and figured it out myself.[13]

He even gives us a formula for preparing this stuff, which is worth repeating here for its curious interest:

Take ten parts of pure gold, ten of silver, five of copper, two of tin, two of lead, one part of powdered iron, and five of mercury. All these metals must be pure. Now wait for the hour when the planets Saturn and Mercury come into conjunction, and have all your preparations ready for that occasion; have the fire, the crucible, the mercury, and the lead ready, so that there will be no delay when the time of the conjunction arrives, for the work must be done during the moments

---

*Which means that the attack itself was probably hysterical.

of the conjunction. As soon as this takes place melt the lead and add the mercury, and let it cool. After this has been done, wait for a conjunction of Jupiter with Saturn and Mercury, melt the compound of mercury and lead in a crucible, and in another crucible the tin, and pour the two metals together at the moment of the conjunction. You must now wait until a conjunction of the Sun with either one or both of the above-named planets takes place, and then add the gold to the compound after melting it previously. At a time of a conjunction of the Moon with the Sun, Saturn, or Mercury, the silver is added likewise, and at a time of a conjunction of Venus with one of the above-named planets the copper is added. Finally, at a time of such a conjunction with Mars, the whole is completed by the addition of powdered iron. Stir the fluid mass with a dry rod of witch-hazel, and let it cool.

Of this electrum magicum you may make a mirror in which you may see the events of the past and present, absent friends or enemies, and see what they are doing. You may see in it any object you may desire to see, and all the doings of men in daytime or at night. You may see in it anything that has ever been written down, said or spoken in the past, and also see the person who said it, and the causes that made him say what he did, and you may see in it anything, however secret it may have been kept.

Such mirrors are made . . . about two inches [in diameter]. They are to be founded at a time when a conjunction of Jupiter and Venus takes place, and moulds made of fine sand are used for that purpose. Grind the mirrors smooth with a grindstone, and polish them with tripoly, and with a piece of wood from a linden tree. All the operations made with the mirror, the grinding, polishing, etc., should take place under favourable planetary aspects, and by selecting the proper hours three different mirrors may be prepared. At a time of a conjunction of two good planets, when at the same time the Sun or the Moon stands on the 'house of the lord of the hour of your birth, the three mirrors are to be laid together into pure well water, and left to remain there for an hour. They may then be removed from the water, enveloped in a linen cloth, and preserved for use.[14]

I would not suggest that you spend a good deal of money trying to make one of these mirrors unless you have some considerable skills as an alchemist, as an astrologer, and as a worker with metals, especially precious metals. It is also obvious, although Paracelsus does not stress this point, that a degree of developed psychic power is necessary to do all the wonderful things he describes with electrum, and some of these can be done almost as well with ordinary mirrors. But the power of the alchemical metals to absorb and trap planetary vibrations should not be underestimated.

Readers of Paramahansa Yogananda's book, *The Autobiography of a Yogi* will notice that very similar ideas are cherished in India, where certain metals and stones are worn on the person to deflect planetary influences and protect the wearer from disease. [15] An Indian yogi may wear an iron bracelet, for example, to absorb the influences of Mars and protect himself from fevers, 'eruptive fevers', and 'diseases of an acute and violent character', since these are all characteristic of the influence of Mars. [16] In her 'Secret Instructions', Madame Blavatsky recommended that her students protect themselves from the Elementals which throng public places . . . by wearing either a ring containing some jewel of the presiding planet, or else of a metal sacred to it,' although she insisted that 'the best protection is a clear conscience and a firm desire to benefit humanity.' [17] The 'presiding planet' is determined by the day of the week and the hour of the day. According to Yogananda, this kind of therapy has often proved almost miraculous when administered by a competent guru with highly developed psychic powers. The Indians and Europeans came to almost identical conclusions about planetary influences and their influence on earthly things, which is not surprising since both of those groups based their theories on psychic experiences. As usual, though, the Easterners have had some interesting insights that seem to have been denied to their more obtuse Western brethren, and these insights have immediate practical applications.

In the last chapter I told you about some yogic methods for assessing the influences of the Sun and the Moon on your astral body. But the Sun and Moon are only two 'planets', astrologically speaking, and there are seven of these planets altogether. To use yogic astrology to maximum effect, you need some additional techniques for evaluating the influences of these other five planets, and the additional insights that I mentioned show us how to develop these additional techniques.

In the 'Secret Instructions' that she prepared for the members of the Esoteric Section of the Theosophical Society, Madame Blavatsky revealed that the left and right nostrils are just two of seven points in the head which correspond to the seven astrological planets. The other points are the two eyes, the two ears and the mouth. It happens that these organs are situated in the human face in such a manner that they form a triangle such as the one we discussed in Chapter Five, thus:

```
RIGHT EYE  .    .    .    .    .    .    .    .    . LEFT EYE

            .                         .

    RIGHT EAR  .              . LEFT EAR

    RIGHT NOSTRIL  .    . LEFT NOSTRIL

                        .

                MOUTH
```

Thus we have the following correspondences between the facial organs, the seven theosophical 'principles', and the seven astrological planets, according to Esoteric Buddhism:

Facial Feature	Astrological Planet	Theosophical Principle
Right Ear	Saturn	Lower Manas
Left Ear	Mars	Kama Rupa
Right Eye	Mercury	Buddhi
Left Eye	Venus	Manas
Right Nostril	Sun	Prana
Left Nostril	Moon	Astral Body
Mouth	Jupiter	Auric Envelope (Atma)

Hindu yogis, as distinguished from their Tibetan counterparts, approach the matter differently. Just as it is no coincidence that there are seven planets and seven metals and seven colours, the yogis insist that it is no coincidence that there are five 'minor' planets and five senses and five 'false' states of matter. They accept the five 'passive' senses of Aristotle, or sight, hearing, tasting, smelling and touching, and add to those five 'active' senses, which they define as speaking, grasping, walking, eliminating, and having sex.[18]

For there to be five senses, of course, there have to be five corresponding things to sense, and these are colour, taste, smell, sound, and resistance. These five sensible objects are related in turn to the five 'false' states of matter: *Akasa, Vayu, Apas, Tejas,* and *Prthivi.*

Now these five 'false' states of matter are also known as the five *Tattwas,* and they correspond roughly to the five 'states' of matter recognized by science, and to the five 'Elements' of the Greeks, thus:

Hindu Tattwa	State of Matter	Greek Element
Akasa	Space	Quintessence
Vayu	Gaseous	Air
Tejas	Fiery	Fire
Apas	Liquid	Water
Prthivi	Solid	Earth

This gives us quite a collection of things that come in fives, and the yogis maintain that there is a subtle connection between these various groups of things which is entirely unknown to the profane and which is not obvious even to the initiated.

In yoga, everything that we can see around us is said to be the gross counterpart of some subtler reality, and it is on the subtler planes that the correspondences we have been speaking of originate. There is no real correspondence or sympathy between the physical metal iron and the physical planet Mars. But there is a correspondence between the *subtle counterpart* of iron and the *subtle counterpart* of Mars, and this correspondence exists because the subtle counterpart of iron and the subtle counterpart of Mars are the same principle. It is obvious that a thing 'corresponds' to itself, and is in 'sympathy' with itself, and the yogic philosophers maintain that one subtle principle can manifest itself materially in three different ways according to which of the three primitive qualities, or *gunas,* predominates.[19]

The 'subtle principles' are known technically in yoga as the *tanmatras.* In the 'Secret Instructions' Madame Blavatsky defines the word 'tanmatra' as meaning 'subtle and rudimentary form, the gross type of the finer elements'.[20] The Maharishi Mahesh Yogi defines them as the grossest form of invisible manifestation. According to which of the three *gunas* predominates, each tanmatra can result in one of three *visible* manifestations, and these three are the Passive Senses, the Active Senses, and the Visible Elements.

The Passive Senses are just the five senses of Aristotle, and in yoga there are of course presumed to be *five* of these Passive Senses because there are five tanmatras from which Passive Senses may be derived.

The Active Senses are, as it were, active counterparts of the Passive Senses. Thus we have Touch as a Passive Sense, and Grasping as an Active Sense, although I must confess the derivation of some of these Active Senses escapes me.

The Visible Elements, or *Mahabhutas*, as they are called in Sanskrit, are just the Five Elements of the Greeks, as I mentioned earlier. Each of these three different types of manifestations can come from just one tanmatra. The relationship between these can perhaps best be shown with a table:

Suble Principle	Passive Sense	Active Sense	Visible Element
(*Tanmatra*)	(*Jnanendriya*)	(*Karmendriya*)	(*Mahabhuta*)
Sabda	Hearing (*Srota*)	Speaking (*Vak*)	Space (*Akasa*)
Sparsa	Touch (*Tvak*)	Grasping (*Pani*)	Air (*Vayu*)
Rupa	Sight (*Caksus*)	Walking (*Pada*)	Fire (*Tejas*)
Rasa	Taste (*Gihva*)	Eliminating (*Payu*)	Water (*Apas*)
Gandha	Smell (*Ghrana*)	Sex (*Upastha*)	Earth (*Prthivi*)

Now the tanmatras in this system correspond to the astral bodies of things in Paracelsus' system, and it is therefore obvious that the tanmatras are the media as it were of the planetary influences. This is completely consistent with the yogic conception of things, and it is important because it gives us a new and crucial fact. *It shows us that the planetary influences affect not only the objects of sense, but the senses themselves.*

You will recall me saying that we must sense the planetary influences, else they would not affect us. According to the yogis, the Active Senses, the Passive Senses, and the Visible Elements are constantly being 'produced', as it were, by processes which operate on the subtle planes and which have to do with the tanmatras.[21] If the planetary vibrations affect the tanmatras in some way, they will indirectly affect the visible manifestations which those tanmatras support, which include the senses, and this is a point which is subject to experimental demons
All of the five senses are in fact affected by all of the fiv
planets, but for practical purposes we shall only be c
with one: the sense of sight.

The tanmatra of sight is *rupa*, which means both colour and form, and it happens that there is a traditional colour and a traditional form associated with each of the five Tattwas. This information may be found in the *Gheranda Samhita* and in certain of the *Yoga Upanishads*.[22] All the Hindu texts are in agreement concerning the proper attributions, although there are some minor disagreements between the Indian and Tibetan manuscripts.[23] We can therefore say that the following seems to be the most authoritative system:

Tattwa	Colour	Form
Akasa	Black	Oval
Vayu	Blue	Circle
Tejas	Red	Triangle
Apas	White	Half Moon
Prthivi	Yellow	Square

The Tattwas would therefore have to be considered a *subtle* principle in nature, and the Golden Dawn manuscripts interpret them as 'currents or sub-planes of the Astral Light' which 'issue in a steady stream from the Sun'.[24] They would therefore have to be considered modifications of the Solar influence, an interpretation which is entirely consistent with all the other principles of yogic astrology. They are said to rotate throughout the day, with the Akasic influence dominating first, followed by the Vayu, the Tejas, Apas and Prthivi; but like the Sun and Moon Breaths, there are better ways to determine which Tattwas are dominant than looking at your watch.

The Solar and Lunar influences affect the way we breathe, but the other planetary influences have a subtle effect on the way we see colours. Each of the Tattwic or planetary influences is attributed to one of five colours, and these five colours are said to be 'very magnetic' because of this. Yogis in Tibet surround themselves with 'the five sacred colours gathered in a circle' while they are meditating.[25] When one or another of the five planetary influences is dominant, it tends to produce a very slight tint in our surroundings corresponding to its attributed colour, and that tint, although never noticed by the average person, can be seen by the trained yogi.

This makes it possible, as the Golden Dawn manuscripts put it, to assess the Tattwas 'not merely by a mathematical calculation, but with the certainty of an eyewitness.'[26] The Golden Dawn lectures tell us to set aside an hour or more 'during the day, when the sky is clear'. We are told to put worldly matters out of our minds, and to stare 'at any part of the blue sky, and go on looking at it without allowing [your eyes] to twinkle.'[27]

Now what this means is that you must practise staring without allowing your eyes to blink. There is an occult reason for this, since blinking is controlled by the *Kurma Vayu*, and it is the gradual subjugation of this vayu which makes it possible for you to stare steadily. This tends to go along with the gradual quieting of the mind, and it has certain occult effects which are not sensed objectively by the yogi, in addition to the reduction of blinking. You must not strain your eyes in any way. Just stare easily, and try very gently to suppress the blinking reflex. If you feel any discomfort resulting from this exercise, you should discontinue it and then try again the following day.

The first effect you will see is 'waves'. They look like heat waves, but yogis maintain that they are actually the Vayu Tattwa, the subtle counterpart of the Water Element in the atmosphere.[28] Scientists would call it atmospheric humidity. This is very easy to see, and you should get this effect during the first or second session with the experiment.

The second effect — which comes to some, but not all — is visions of people, cities, and so forth. This comes to people who have some natural clairvoyance. In his *Yoga, Youth, and Reincarnation*, Jess Stearn says that staring at a candle flame starts up the same kinds of visions for some people. After these visions have come and gone, if you are successful, you will begin to see colours, and this is of course the object of the exercise.

The Golden Dawn manuscripts say that the colours at first will be 'mixed', but that is just a way of saying that they are uncertain.[29] It is difficult to put into words exactly how one experiences this, so I shall leave it to the reader to find out for himself. Suffice it to say that, with practice, the colours will become definite enough that you should be able to identify which Tattwa and which of the corresponding planetary influences happens to be dominant at that given moment in time. On that basis, you may be able to determine whether the purely astrological conditions are favourable to this or that activity which you might be contemplating.

Now there are, as I have said, five of these astrological influences which we have not yet discussed. Hence, to give you an idea what each of the colours you might see could mean, let us examine the nature of these influences as they are described in traditional astrological sources.

Akasa

Akasa corresponds in Hindu philosophy to the Quintessence of the Greeks. It is the First Matter of the alchemists, from which all other matter originates, which is why it is always given first in the 'order of subtle emanation'. It is the most subtle of the five material principles, and it is *so* subtle that laymen tend to think of it as empty space, although of course there is no such thing. Its seat in the human body, according to the principles of Kundalini Yoga, is the area of the throat, which is the seat of the psychic centre known as the *Visuddha Chakra*. Since it corresponds to the sense of hearing, its associated form is said in the Golden Dawn manuscripts to be an oval of the shape of the human ear. The influence of Akasa is known to the Adept when he sees the 'colour' black.

It is worth mentioning here that black, when it appears in the human aura, is the colour of despair and depression. The vibrations associated with this colour are of a low order, and this phenomenon is particularly easy to see, even in bright daylight, which obscures other auric colours. It appears much like a black cloud hovering over the head of the afflicted person, and it seems certain that this is the origin of the saying that depressed people have a 'cloud' hanging over them. This is why the 'blues' are sometimes called 'the black mood'. Winston Churchill spoke of the depression that haunted him throughout much of his life as his 'black dog'. Black is also the colour of hate.

In alchemy, black is the colour of the planet Saturn, which is usually thought of as a negative influence. *The Key of Solomon* therefore recommends it 'to bring destruction and give death, and to sow hatred and discord.' Mouni Sadhu says that 'on the physical plane' Saturn 'dictates material experiences, melancholy moods, anxiety, and often extreme parsimony.'[30]

The Key also recommends the days ruled by Saturn for 'experiments to summon the souls from Hades, but only of those who have died a natural death.' Those who died violently are to be summoned under the influence of Mars. These days are also recommended for operations 'to bring either good or bad fortune to buildings, to have familiar spirits attend to thee in sleep, [and] to cause good or ill success to business, possessions, goods, seeds, fruits, and similar things.'

Paracelsus says that 'to Saturn belongs especially that which is concerned with mines and the digging of ground.' This suggests that periods ruled by Saturn are favourable to such activities as mining, excavation, archaeological explorations, plowing, planting crops, erecting fences, and searching for buried treasure, since all these things involve 'the digging of ground.'

Vayu

Vayu is the subtle counterpart of the Air Element, and its psychic colour is blue. In fact, its proper colour is *sky* blue, and it is said that we see blue when we look into the sky because of the vast expanse of Vayu surrounding us.[31] Its seat in the human body is the heart, which is the location of the *Anahat Chakra*. When Vayu is dominant, it tends to produce a slight bluish tint in the human aura, and this tends to tint one's perceptions of one's surroundings very slightly — an effect which can be seen by psychically sensitive persons.

Leadbeater says that when dark blue appears in the human aura it represents religious devotion, whereas lighter shades refer to nobility and faith. In fact, blue is used in colour therapy because it is a 'cool' colour, and because it is soothing to the nervous system.[32]

In his little pamphlet on *Auras* Edgar Cayce says that light blue indicates 'little depth', whereas dark blue is the colour of a person who has made a commitment to whatever it is he is doing in life, 'usually . . . an unselfish cause . . . I have seen many Sisters of Mercy with this dark blue, and writers and singers also.'

In alchemy, blue corresponds to the influence of the planet Jupiter, which is the most benign of all the astrological influences. According to *The Key of Solomon*, those days which are ruled by Jupiter are 'proper for obtaining honours, acquiring riches, contracting friendships, preserving health, and arriving at all that thou canst desire.' The *hours* of Jupiter, Venus, and the Sun are 'adapted for preparing any operation whatsoever of love, of kindness, and of *invisibility*,' and 'for all extraordinary, uncommon, and unknown operations.' Paracelsus says that 'Jupiter governs the courts of law [and] churches', from which we may infer that Jupiter's influence is favourable for dealing with judges, or with lawyers, for the preparation of contracts, wills, and other legal documents, for bringing cases before the bar, and for dealing with clergymen, for contracting marriage, or for pondering ethical, moral, and spiritual questions. Edgar Cayce connects Jupiter with 'the great ennobling conditions; those which would bring money and the influence for good into the life.'[33]

Tejas

Tejas is the subtle counterpart of the Fire Element, and is known to be dominant when the Adept sees the colour red. In the human body it is seated in the region of the solar plexus, where is located the *Manipura Chakra*, the seat of the *Samana Vayu*, which is the *fire* of digestion. It is worth noting here that this 'fire' is quite real, and not metaphorical. Properly awakened, it is recommended by Patanjali in *The Yoga Sutras* for intensifying the human aura, so that it becomes visible in a darkened room.[34] It is also the basis for the Tibetan practice of *tumo*, in which the yogi generates sufficient internal heat to bathe naked in freezing water without discomfort.[35] Tejas is said to be auspicious for 'harsh acts' and acts which 'set one on fire.'[36] When it is dominant the body tends to be somewhat warmer than at other times. If the Adept falls ill when Tejas is dominant, he will tend to have those diseases in which there is fever and trembling, all of which are consistent with the idea of Fire.[37]

Tejas tends to produce a reddish tinge in our colour perception, and it also tends slightly to redden the human aura, hence the old expression that one is 'seeing red' when angry. According to Edgar Cayce, this colour 'indicates force, vigour, and energy.' Whereas black is the colour of depression and hate, dark red is the colour of anger. It is an extremely invigorating colour, and timid people are generally reluctant to wear red for that reason.

In alchemy, red corresponds to the influence of the planet Mars, and Paracelsus says that Mars rules 'all that is concerned with war, arms, and ammunitions.' *The Key of Solomon* recommends the days dominated by Mars for 'experiments regarding war, to arrive at military honour, to acquire courage, to overthrow enemies, and further to cause ruin, slaughter, cruelty, [and] discord, to wound and to give death.' Not a very kind-hearted influence. The hours of Mars are said to 'serve for the summoning of souls from Hades, especially of those slain in battle.'

Thus we would expect periods dominated by Mars to be in many ways the opposite of those dominated by the Sun. Both the Solar and Martial influences are serviceable for dealing with enemies, but whereas the Solar influence favours efforts at diplomacy and reconciliation, Mars is more favourable to efforts at conquest and domination. Logically, we would expect that Mars would be excellent for pursuing lawsuits, for dealing with collection agencies, for military matters, and similar activities, but would be unfavourable for diplomatically-oriented activities such as seeking favours, contracting marriage, or working out agreements of any kind, for negotiations, or for signing legal papers.

Apas

Apas is the subtle counterpart of the Water Element, and is known to be dominant when the Adept sees white. In alchemy, white is the colour of the planet Mercury, thus those periods when Apas is dominant would be excellent for things which have to do with the understanding. *The Key of Solomon* says the days ruled by Mercury 'are good to operate for eloquence and intelligence, promptitude in business, science and divination, wonders, apparitions, and answers regarding the future' as well as 'thefts, writings, deceits, and merchandise.' It is an intellectual period and gives great impetus to the mind. The hours of Mercury are said to be 'good for undertaking experiments relating to games, raillery, jests, sports, and the like.' In the human body, it corresponds to the *Svadisthana Chakra*, which is located in the vicinity of the genital organs.

Prthivi

Prthivi is the subtle counterpart of the Earth Element. Astrologically, it corresponds to the influence of the planet Venus, and *The Key of Solomon* recommends 'the days and hours of Venus' for 'forming friendships, for kindness and love, for joyous and pleasant undertakings, and for travelling.' The *hours* of Venus are specifically recommended for 'lots, poisons, for preparing powders provocative of madness, and the like.' Paracelsus says 'Venus rules that which belongs to music [and] sexual attractions.' from which we could infer that the periods ruled by Venus would be favourable to the study of music, for dealing with persons of the opposite sex in either a friendly or a romantic fashion, for contracting marriages, and for parties.

In the human body Prthivi is said to be seated in the *Muladhara Chakra*, which is situated at the base of the spine and is the physical origin of the mystical energy known as *Kundalini*. This is significant because students of Kundalini Yoga report that the first stirrings of that energy produce visions of an erotic nature, and this is of course one of the characteristics of the Venusian influence.[38]

The colour yellow, though, which the yogis say is the proper colour of Prthivi, is not Venusian at all. Yellow is a soothing colour, and is considered an excellent colour for sleeping apparel, for linens, and for draperies to be used in sleeping rooms. Leadbeater says that yellow is the colour seen in the aura of an intellectual, which would be the correct colour for Mercury but definitely not for Venus. Green, though, which is attributed to Venus in Western alchemy, *is* Venusian. Leadbeater says several different shades are found in the human aura. Green-brown is the colour of jealousy, whereas grey-green is the colour of deceit and cunning. Emerald green denotes versatility and ingenuity, whereas pale, delicate green signifies sympathy and compassion. All these attributes are normally associated with romantic love, although let it be said that green is soothing, and not an arousing colour. In colour therapy green is used for high blood-pressure, nervous problems, rapid heartbeat, and fevers.

If meditation and yoga are not to your taste, though, there is another system which you may use which does not produce as precise results as yoga systems, but which does give some very valuable insights indeed. It requires no psychic development whatever to use, it was left to us by Jerome Cardan, and it is the topic we shall take up next.

8

Jerome Cardan's System

If you believe in astrology, there is a way of making use of astrological principles to improve your luck which requires no psychic development on your part whatever. It is somewhat less precise than the yoga methods, but it can produce results which are 'truly remarkable', to borrow Littlewood's phrase and, like the yoga methods, it requires no horoscopes, no charts, and no spherical trigonometry. It is simplicity itself, and it was left to us by the medieval astrologer Jerome Cardan.

According to Eliphas Levi, who describes the system in his *Dogme et rituel de la haute magie,* Cardan

> based his theory upon his own experiences, and assured us that the calculation never failed him. To know then that which will be the fortune of a given year, he sums the events of those [years] which preceded it by 4, 8, 12, 19, and 30. The number 4 is that of realization. The number 8, that of Venus or of natural things. The number 12, which is that of the cycle of Jupiter, corresponds to successes. To the number 19 corresponds the cycles of the Moon, and of Mars. The number 30 is that of Saturn or of Fatality.
>
> Thus, for example, I would know that which will come to me in this year, 1855. I pass in my memory over events which were decisive and real in the order of progress and of life four years ago, that which I had of good fortune or natural bad luck eight years ago, that which I have counted of success or of misfortune twelve years ago, the vicissitudes and the evil hours or the maladies which came to me nineteen years ago, and that which tragically or fatally tested me

thirty years ago. Then, in taking count of irrevocable accomplished facts and of the progress of age, I count on the chances analogous to those which I owe already to the influences of the same planets, and I say: in 1851 I had an occupation which was mediocre but sufficiently lucrative, with some embarrassment of position. In 1847 I was violently separated from my family, and the result of this separation was great suffering for myself and mine. In 1843, I voyaged as an apostle, speaking to the people and persecuted by gentlemen of ill intentions: I was, in two words, honoured and proscribed. Finally in 1825, family life ceased for me, and I engaged myself definitively in the fatal path which conducted me to science and evil times. I may then believe that this year I will have work, poverty, torment, an exile of the heart, change of place, publicity, and contradictions — events decisive for the rest of my existence. And I find already in the present all sorts of reasons to believe in this future. I therefore conclude for myself and for the present year that experience perfectly confirms the justice of the astrological calculations of Cardan.[1]

My own experience with this system 'perfectly confirms the justice of the astrological calculations of Cardan' as well. Looking back over the years, I can see how, if I had known of this system earlier, I could have taken advantage of opportunities that I let slide, and at the same time foreseen pitfalls that I fell into.

To make this system as easy as possible for you to use, I have prepared the following chart, on which you can see the planetary cycles for every year from the year of writing to the end of this century.

Present	−4	−8	−12	−19	−30
1983	1979	1975	1971	1964	1953
1984	1980	1976	1972	1965	1954
1985	1981	1977	1973	1966	1955
1986	1982	1978	1974	1967	1956
1987	1983	1979	1975	1968	1957
1988	1984	1980	1976	1969	1958
1989	1985	1981	1977	1970	1959
1990	1986	1982	1978	1971	1960
1991	1987	1983	1979	1972	1961
1992	1988	1984	1980	1973	1962
1993	1989	1985	1981	1974	1963
1994	1990	1986	1982	1975	1964
1995	1991	1987	1983	1976	1965

Present	−4	−8	−12	−19	−30
1996	1992	1988	1984	1977	1966
1997	1993	1989	1985	1978	1967
1998	1994	1990	1986	1979	1968
1999	1995	1991	1987	1980	1969
2000	1996	1992	1988	1981	1970

The easiest way for you for see how it works, and decide for yourself if it has value for you, is to take some year of your life that has already gone by, and try to interpret it in terms of the system. For example, by the time you read this, 1983 will have already gone by. Using the following chart, you can easily see that four years before 1983 was 1979, eight years before was 1975, twelve years before was 1971, nineteen years before was 1964, and thirty years before was 1953. These years correspond to Mercury, Venus, Jupiter, the Moon and Mars, and Saturn respectively.

Now Mercury has to do with intellectual things, and operates according to Cardan on a four year cycle. Let us suppose that in 1979 you achieved something in the intellectual area. You could have completed an academic course, won a diploma, mastered some difficult subject, gained some great insight — *anything*, so long as it was intellectual in character *and* was not something that you do every year. The fact that you were able to complete it successfully suggests that the planets might have been favourable to similar projects four years later in 1983.

Now bear in mind here that what we are looking for is not just some run-of-the-mill incident, but something unusual and distinctive, which happened in 1979 and which seems to betray signs of the Mercurial influence. If you are a college graduate, it may be that you acquired your diploma in 1979. Or perhaps the influence was negative. Perhaps there was a period during this year when you had difficulty concentrating, or when you felt you were under unusual stress. In that case, you may have been vulnerable to something similar in 1983, and it may be that this cycle should be taken as a warning.

Then again it may be that 1979 was an insignificant year so far as Mercury is concerned. If nothing unusually interesting happened to you in that year, and you had no unusually interesting moments of intellectual good or bad fortune in that year, then it probably happened that 1983 was also neutral for you, at least insofar as Mercury is concerned. If you believe that 1979 *was* significant in some way, then think back over 1983 and see if you can't see how the influences which shaped 1979 recurred four years later. You may be surprised to see that your personal history repeated itself. And then agan you may see that you missed certain opportunities which you could have prudently taken advantage of had you had the information in this system.

You may also notice another pattern of a less advantageous character if you are the type who scouts about for business ventures, speculations, investments, and such things as that. According to the writer of *The Key of Solomon*, Mercury is the planet which has to do with 'thefts and deceptions', and if business opportunities are destined to cross your desk which are put together with perhaps less than honourable intent, they will do so at intervals of just about four years. In my own experience, I see that I was enticed into a limited partnership for land speculation in 1973 which turned out on close inspection to have been of a perhaps questionable nature. With that in mind it is obvious that, if Cardan is right, I should have had similar 'opportunities' come my way in 1977 and 1981, but not in 1974, 1975, 1976, 1978, 1979, or 1980 — and this was in fact the case. Carrying this into the future, I can see that as 1985 unfolds I shall have to be more vigilant than usual and even suspicious in checking out business opportunities that may present themselves, and this information has already proved useful even though as I am writing this it is now only the early part of January.

Eight years before 1983 was 1975, and that year, says Cardan, has to do with 'Venus, or natural things'. Now 'natural things' is a nineteenth-century way of saying sexual things, and we find that Venus rules all sexual and romantic matters, including marriage, as well as matters having to do with gaiety, music, and so forth. It is no coincidence that *seven* is the average number of years a marriage lasts — hence the old saying about the 'seven year itch' — and that divorcees usually remarry in the *eighth* year.

Therefore, think back to 1975 and ask yourself if there was not some significant incident or incidents which had to do with things ruled by Venus. Perhaps you took up the study of music, perhaps you married, began a love affair, or renewed an old one. There are all sorts of possibilities. Then bring yourself back mentally to 1983 and see if there was not some cyclic repetition of those events, perhaps masquerading as 'new' events, but really just a repetition of the past. As with the Mercurial influence, there may not have been anything outstandingly Venusian about 1975. However, if there was, you should be able to detect the cyclic influences at work eight years later.

Thinking back to 1971, bear in mind that this year has to do with the cycles of Jupiter. Was there anything particularly Jupiterian about 1971, and, if so, can you see how that influence may have made itself felt in your life in 1983? Cardan says Jupiter has to do with 'successes'. Did you enjoy any striking successes twelve years ago, and if so, what areas of your life did they occur in? Did you obtain honours, acquire riches, contract friendships, preserve health, and arrive 'at all thou canst desire?' If so — and bear in mind that we are talking about unusual things here, striking, significant events — then look back over 1983. Did you repeat your experience of 1971 in that year? And if not, were there any opportunities that you may have missed perhaps because of excessive conservatism? This kind of exercise with regard to the past will help you greatly in predicting the opportunities and hazards that will befall you in the future.

Nineteen years before 1983 was 1964, the year of the Moon and Mars, and thirty years before 1983 was 1953, the year of Saturn and Fatality. In both these cases, you will want to review the descriptions of the planetary influences for these three planets, and see if you can remember anything that happened in those years which seems significant to you and which seems to suggest the influence of those particular planets.

If you are not much over thirty, you may find it difficult to remember things which happened thirty years ago, or even nineteen years ago. I have no recollection at all of 1953, although I can remember 1964 fairly well. If this is your situation as well, you might want to start a diary in which you note events of unusual importance that you might want to be able to place accurately in time years from now. If you do not want to spend the time to work on a diary (and they do take time), then you might want to save letters, souvenirs, and other items which have dates written on them. You will find it quite difficult seven or eight years from now to remember in what year this or that occurred with any accuracy, and accuracy is precisely what you will need to use this system effectively.

Another way that you can test this system is to apply it to historical events. This is much more difficult to do accurately, since there are so many things happening in the world at any given time, and any conclusions one could reach are debatable, but it can be done. The cycles work for entire societies as well as individuals. In the USA, people who follow these things have pointed out that there seems to be a 'twenty year cycle' which governs the deaths of American Presidents. Nineteen years is the cycle of the planet Mars, which governs assassinations, wars and such like, but there is a one-year discrepancy between this cycle ordained by nature and the artificial one ordained by the American Constitution. Presidents are elected every four years, and Presidents who have been elected at twenty-year intervals tend to die in office. The chain of coincidences is not perfect, but it is impressive. And some there are who think it may betray evidence of astrological influences.

Abraham Lincoln was elected in 1860, and was shot fatally by John Wilkes Booth on 15 April 1865. James A. Garfield was elected in 1880 and was shot on 2 July 1881 by Charles J. Guiteau, a mentally deranged man who, it turned out, was unhappy about his inability to secure a federal appointment. Garfield died on 19 September 1881. Chester Arthur took over from Garfield and died on 18 November 1886 from Bright's disease. He is a partial exception, since he would have died in office, had he not failed to win the 1884 election. A clear exception is Theodore Roosevelt, who was elected in 1900, but who did not die until 6 January 1919, long after he was out of power. After Roosevelt, though, the deadly cycle seems to have begun again.

Warren G. Harding was elected in 1920 and died in San Francisco in August 1923, on his return from a journey to Alaska. Franklin Roosevelt was elect in 1940 and died of natural causes on 12 April 1945, just about a month before the Germans surrendered to the Allies. John F. Kennedy was elected in 1960, and was assassinated on 22 November 1963. Had it not been for sheer luck, Ronald Reagan would have added further confirmation to the apparent efficacy of this grim cycle. He was elected in 1980 and was then shot by John Hinckley in Washington, D.C., but in this case two extraordinary instances of good luck seem to have saved his life: first, the 'Devastator' bullet which was used by his would-be assassin failed to explode after entering his body, and second, as soon as it hit him it was miraculously deflected by his seventh rib, turning it away from his vital organs. Hopefully, you will not be shot by anyone, but if you are destined to have trouble with enemies, you may find that trouble manifesting itself at nineteen-year intervals.

The system is so simple, it is difficult for the human mind to accept the fact that it works, but work it surely does, and all you have to do to prove it is keep accurate notes on the things that happen to you over the years.

Now I want to introduce you to one more divination system that requires even less effort than Cardan's — and yet which works even better for some people. It not only requires no psychic development and no horoscopes, but it does not even require a diary. It requires almost nothing on the part of the user except interest. And with skill you may dispense with even that.

9

I See by the Book

There is a mode of divination which seems to be neglected today, but which was once used very widely, and which requires no psychic powers and no study whatsoever to use. It is the essence of simplicity itself, and yet those who have experimented with it for even a short time have found it to be an infallible guide to their daily affairs. The technical name for it is *biblomancy*.

That may seem like a mouthful, but actually the word biblomancy is derived from *biblio*, which means 'book', and *mancy*, which means 'divination'. It is literally 'divination by means of a book', and here is how it is done.

You need a book of wisdom. You may use a family Bible if you have one, or you may use some similar book which contains wisdom sayings that are short and to the point. Ralph Houston, the famous *Guru* of Agni Yoga, used the books in the Agni Yoga series.[1] In England during the Middle Ages people used Virgil's *Aeneid*, since he had a reputation for being not merely a poet but a sorcerer as well. King Charles I is said to have foreseen his own untimely death by hanging when performing biblomancy with this book. You might want to use one of the old books of proverbs that were popular years ago and that can still be found in antiquarian bookshops from time to time. But *whatever* you use, it should be a book which is designed to give counsel and which does so in a very concise manner. This shall be your divinatory instrument.

Once you have selected it, you must hold it in your hands for a moment and think intently of the question you want to ask. It can be as vague as you wish, but you should be fair to the oracle and not make it unreasonably precise. You may, for example, ask the oracle if you should change jobs or not, but don't ask it for the name of the company you should work for. If you do not have a question in mind, then just ask for some word of wise counsel which will be appropriate for this particular moment in your life. This is an excellent practice with which to start your day. Then open the book at random and read the *first passage* you see, and try to interpret it in terms of the question you have in mind.

That is all! It is difficult to see how such a simple technique could have any value to it, but if you stay with it for a while you will get results with this that are astonishing indeed. In fact, this principle of interpreting a seemingly random event is the basis for almost all systems of divination.

It was on this basis that Jung came up with his famous theory of 'Synchronicity'. People who practise divination assume that chance occurrences are somehow meaningful, even though they appear outwardly to be merely random accidents. This is the same feeling that comes over more hard-headed types when they see a truly striking coincidence – the feeling that a coincidence sometimes may be more than *just* a coincidence. Hence, Jung coined the phrase 'meaningful coincidence', meaning that it *may* be a coincidence, but that it conceals some kind of meaning anyway.

The phrase 'meaningful coincidence' seems to be something of an oxymoron, though – like 'government efficiency', or 'military intelligence'. It is a concatenation of two words with meanings that seem to be mutually exclusive. So to disguise the slightly questionable character of the idea, Jung coined a single word for the phenomenon which has stood the test of time better than 'meaningful coincidence'. He called the underlying principle behind these kinds of coincidences *synchronicity.*

In the August of 1983 the Association for Research and Enlightenment in Virginia Beach, Virginia, put this notion of 'synchronicity' to a truly scientific test. It must be said here that the ARE has a much more scientific attitude toward psychic phenomena than other organizations of the same type, and organizes several research projects every year in which their members are invited to take part. Moreover, they are not unwilling to publish even negative results, which gives their experiments more credibility than even those of some parapsychology laboratories.

According to one of the Edgar Cayce theories at a certain profound level all the events of one's life are unified by what the ARE literature calls 'the primary connectedness of all things — what we might call the law of oneness.' Thus 'a typical person might look at her life and say that there is no connection between her child, her secretary at work, a person met randomly in the bank, and what appears on a late-night television show.' Yet these are all 'aspects of her experience in a typical day' and 'the law of oneness . . . says that at a more profound level all these parts of her life may be related.' When uncanny coincidences manifest themselves, the ARE says that this principle of oneness has manifested itself in one's experience in what they describe as 'a primary way.'[2]

Put that way, the principle of synchronicity seems much more credible than it does when Jung describes it, and the ARE suggests a way in which it could manifest itself. Suppose the woman just mentioned overhears her child talking about fishing at breakfast. Then her secretary asks for a day off to go fishing. Then she strikes up a conversation with a man in a bank queue, only to discover that his profession is arranging deep-sea fishing trips. Then that night, she listens to a talk show on television, and the topic is fishing. The essential oneness which supposedly exists at a profound level between her child, her secretary, her bank, and her favourite television programme has found expression in an unusual coincidence, and thereby called her attention to itself although theoretically, it was there all the time.

Applied to biblomancy, this would suggest an 'essential oneness' between the act of opening a book at random, and the random occurrence of events later in one's day. It is a very attractive theory, and to test it, the ARE proposed one of their 'Membership Research Projects' to their members.

Participating members were asked to choose one of twelve 'Consciousness Principles' for each of twelve days. The twelve days did not have to be consecutive. The member could skip a day if he or she wished to do so. But each day was to have only one 'Consciousness Principle', and each 'Consciousness Principle' was to be used for only one day.

The recommended mode of selection was to write the numbers

one to twelve on twelve slips of paper, and then put those into a box, and select one each day at random. Then, the participant was asked to keep the associated 'Consciousness Principle' in mind throughout the rest of the day and watch for possibly synchronistic coincidences. The Consciousness Principles were taken from the Edgar Cayce psychic readings and paraphrased for the project. Typical Consciousness Principles were 'The value of laughter' and 'The importance of accepting others.' The frequency of synchronistic occurrences was to be recorded for each day.

Oddly enough, some of the participants noticed synchronistic occurrences, but the day *after* the day on which the Consciousness Principle was adopted. The ARE researchers compared this with a 'a well known displacement phenomenon in ESP research, in which a subject's guesses have a high level of accuracy if applied to the subsequent target.'[3] Other participants noticed dream experiences in which the Consciousness Principle appeared in one form or another.

The object of the experiment was to show that certain kinds of Consciousness Principles were more likly to produce synchronistic experiences than others, and this hypothesis was not supported by the statistical evidence. But the 'anecdotal accounts included on participants' report forms' did lend some credence to the concept of synchronicity. The researchers described some of them as 'remarkable.'[4]

Another explanation of synchronicity-type experiences that may be more pleasing to some of my readers was proposed by Jung's more materialistic teacher, Sigmund Freud. In his *Psychopathology of Everyday Life*, Freud assumes that the way we see the world reflects our own interior psychological state. Thus, coincidences can sometimes tell us something because our own minds sometimes participate in making the coincidences happen.

He gives an example. One of his patients was more than ninety years old, and he had naturally had thoughts more than once that she might not be his patient (or anyone else's) much longer. One day he took a carriage to her house, and the driver stopped by mistake at another house which was amazingly similar in appearance to her house, and which was at the very same street number, but on a different street. A superstitious person, he says, would have seen in this an omen of the old woman's imminent demise.

But Freud saw no significance in this only because his own unconscious mental processes did not seem to be involved. Had he *walked* to the woman's house, and arrived at another house by mistake, he says that one could argue his unconscious mind made the 'mistake' deliberately — as an expression of its concern for the woman's health.[5] Thus 'the Roman who gave up an important undertaking because he sighted an ill-omened flock of birds was relatively right' in his opinion; 'his action was consistent with his principles. But if he withdrew from an undertaking because he had stumbled on his threshold, he was absolutely superior even to us unbelievers ... His stumbling could demonstrate to him the existence of a doubt, an internal counter-current, the force of which could weaken the power of his intention at the moment of its execution.'[6] This is undoubtedly part of the reason why consulting one's nostrils works in the Far East with such legendary success, and it could be the basis for the success of biblomancy as well.

Of course, the interpretation was around long before Freud. In his *Dogme et rituel de la haute magie*, Eliphas Levi suggests that 'all cabalistic and astrological calculations' acquire 'value and reality' entirely from 'magnetic intuitions,' and he proposes that 'if [these calculations are] made without inspiration, by cold curiosity and without a powerful will' they are 'perhaps puerile and completely arbitrary.'[7]

In *My Rosicrucian Adventure* Israel Regardie argues that divination methods of every type 'serve in actual practice only as a basis for the working of the inner faculties.' They 'stimulate, as few exercises can, the faculties of clairvoyance, imagination, and intuition,' faculties which 'in most people' are 'wholly dormant', and they 'provide for them a thrust-block as it were from which they may "kick-off".'[8] According to this interpretation, the book you use in biblomancy has no real significance in itself, but is merely an instrument for bringing out your own latent powers.

If you prefer something more elaborate than merely opening a book, there are ways of accommodating your tastes.

In 1867 Paschal Beverly Randolph published an 'Ancient Kaldi Oracle', or 'Rosicrucian Predictive Symph', which he claimed to have 'translated from original Rosicrucian tablets.' The language in this 'symph' is typical of the kind of purple prose for which Randolph was famous, which makes me sceptical that the oracle was 'ancient', or that it was 'Kaldi', or that it was 'translated from the original Rosicrucian Tablets'. Particularly the word 'translated' used in connection with the word 'Tablets' in 1867 suggests that Randolph might have been imitating Joseph Smith, who was active at that time. But ancient or not, the 'Ancient Kaldi Oracle' is obviously a biblomantic system, dressed up slightly for the benefit of those who are doubtful of extremely simple ideas.

To use this oracle, you take seven playing cards with face values of 1 to 7. It does not matter if they are all of the same suit, but they should all have different face values, and they should be indistinguishable from each other if viewed from the back. The instructions which come with the 'Ancient Kaldi Oracle' suggest that you cut out your own cards from slips of paper but, for the reasons aforementioned, manufactured cards work better. You hold all seven cards 'in the palm of the left hand with the right hand resting lightly upon them,' and meditate for a moment on the question you have in mind. Then you set the cards on the table before you, face down, and 'mix them well'. Once you have done that, you face the East, 'and gently wave your hand over the table' for a few moments with the thought in mind that you will feel 'impelled to touch the card that will answer your question correctly'. If you do feel so 'impelled', you may turn over the card in question and look up your answer in a list which comes with the instructions. If the card you have selected is an ace, your answer is:

> 'Yes. Truth compels a strangely potent yes!
> The hovering Fates your onward pathway bless.'

This is what I mean by 'purple prose'. Somehow the letter 'Y' would seem to me to have been sufficient. Some of the advice is more ambiguous, though, and gives more play to your budding psychic powers. A five, for example, gives you the following sage counsel:

> 'A good day blackens into a gloomy night
> Beware a fall, a woman tall, a quarrel and a fight.'

Or this for the number two:

> 'Beware, a snare — the tiger's lair — take care — forbear
> Awhile, then triumph comes. Be wise. Prepare!'

One gets the impression that Randolph started out in life writing fortune cookies for Chinese restaurants.

Another system of this type is *Napoleon's Book of Fate*, although the quality of the advice is slightly higher. To use this *oraculum* you must draw five rows of vertical lines at random, and without actually counting them, you must be fairly sure that there are more than twelve lines in each of the five rows. After that is done, you must count the number of lines in each row and subtract twelve. Thus if you find that you have drawn fifteen lines on the first row, you must subtract twelve from that, and you have three left over. Three is an odd number, so you write down one star. If the number had been even, you would write down two stars. This process is repeated for each of the five rows until you have something that looks like this:

```
        *
*       *
*       *
        *
        *
```

Then you simply look in the oraculum for the query which seems to most closely resemble the question that you have in mind. Typical queries are 'Will the marriage be prosperous?' and 'Will she have a son or daughter?', although there are others of more general character, such as 'Shall I be lucky or unlucky this day?' or 'What does my dream signify?' Once you have selected the query which seems most appropriate, you turn to the section which has answers related to that query, and, using the constellation of stars you have written down, you find your answer.

Suppose your question was 'Shall I live to an old age?' According to one version of the oraculum, the answer for the constellation that I have drawn above is 'Drunkenness brings on premature old age; avoid it and you will live long.' Since I am a teetotaller, that would seem to mean 'yes'.

This is a very attractive book, and is available in several editions, all of which are essentially reprints of versions published early in the nineteenth century. Thousands of people have used it for biblomancy ever since its namesake was careering across Europe. However, I find I get better results using a Bible, or, better yet, an *I Ching*.

This last system requires no introduction. It is an ancient Chinese system of divination in which one throws coins or yarrow stalks in order to figure out how to open a book of Confucian advice on matters of life. The coins and yarrow stalks are, of course, irrelevant. They serve only to conceal the fact that one is opening a book at random — as in any other system of biblomancy. But the *book* in this case is one that is truly remarkable. It is infinitely superior to Randolph's 'Ancient Kaldi Oracle' and much superior even to *Napoleon's Book of Fate*. In his *Powers of Mind*, Adam Smith describes an astonishing experiment in which the *I Ching* was used to pick stock prices with the aid of a computer. But the best story of the *I Ching* I have ever seen comes from Japan, where the system has been in use since ancient times. It appears in a very old book by Lafcadio Hearn — *In Ghostly Japan*— and it is of sufficient interest that it seems appropriate to end this chapter with it.

I once knew a fortune teller who really believed in the science that he professed. He had learned, as a student of the old Chinese philosophy, to believe in divination long before he thought of practising it. During his youth he had been in the service of a wealthy *daimyo*, but subsequently, like thousands of other samurai, found himself reduced to desperate straits by the social and political changes of Meiji. It was then that he became a fortune teller, an itinerant *uranaiya*, travelling on foot from town to town, and returning to his home rarely more than once a year with the proceeds of his journey. As a fortune teller, he was tolerably successful, chiefly, I think, because of his perfect sincerity, and because of a peculiar gentle manner that invited confidence. His system was the old scholarly one; he used the book known to English readers as the *I Ching*, also a set of ebony blocks which could be so arranged as to form any of the Chinese hexagrams; and he always began his divination with an earnest prayer to the gods.

The system itself he held to be infallible in the hands of a master. He confessed that he had made some erroneous predictions; but he said that these mistakes had been entirely due to his own miscomprehension of certain texts or diagrams. To do him justice I must mention that in my own case (he told my fortune four times) his predictions were fulfilled in such wise that I became afraid of them. You may disbelieve in fortune-telling, intellectually scorn it; but something of inherited superstitious tendency lurks within most of us; and a few strange experiences can so appeal to that inheritance as to induce the most unreasoning hope or fear of the good or bad luck promised you by some diviner. Really to see our future would be a misery. Imagine the result of knowing that there must happen to you, within the next two months, some terrible misfortune that you cannot possibly provide against!

He was already an old man when I first saw him in Izumo, certainly more than sixty years of age, but looking very much younger. Afterwards, I met him in Osaka, in Kyoto, and in Kobe. More than once I tried to persuade him to pass the colder months of the winter season under my roof; for he possessed an extraordinary knowledge of traditions, and could have been of inestimable service to me in a literary way. But partly because the habit of wandering had become with him a second nature, and partly because of a love of independence as savage as a gipsy's, I was never able to keep him with me for more than two days at a time.

Every year he used to come to Tokyo, usually in the latter part of autumn. Then, for several weeks, he would flit about the city, from district to district, and vanish again. But during these fugitive trips he never failed to visit me; bringing welcome news of Izumo people and places, bringing also some queer little present, generally of a religious kind, from some famous place of pilgrimage. On these occasions I could get a few hours' chat with him. Sometimes the talk was of strange things seen or heard during his recent journey; sometimes it turned upon old legends or beliefs; sometimes it was about fortune-telling. The last time we met he told me of an exact Chinese science of divination which he regretted never having been able to learn.

'Anyone learned in that science,' he said, 'would be able, not only to tell you the exact time at which any post or beam of this house will yield to decay, but even to tell you the direction of the breaking and all its results. I can best explain what I mean by relating a story.

'The story is about the famous Chinese fortune teller whom we call in Japan Shoko Setsu, and it is written in the book *Baikwa-Shin-Eki*, which is a book of divination. While still a very young man, Shoko Setsu obtained a high position by reason of his learning and virtue; but he resigned it and went into solitude that he might give his whole time to study. For years thereafter he lived alone in a hut among the mountains; studying without a fire in winter, and without a fan in summer; writing his thoughts upon the wall of his room — for lack of paper; and using only a tile for his pillow.

'One day, in the period of greatest summer heat, he found himself overcome by drowsiness; and he lay down to rest, with his tile under his head. Scarcely had he fallen asleep when a rat ran across his face and woke him with a start. Feeling angry, he seized his tile and flung it at the rat, but the rat escaped unhurt, and the tile was broken.

Shoko Setsu looked sorrowfully at the fragments of his pillow, and reproached himself for his hastiness. Then suddenly he perceived upon the freshly exposed clay of the broken tile some Chinese characters — between the upper and lower surfaces. Thinking this very strange, he picked up the pieces, and carefully examined them. He found that along the line of fracture seventeen characters had been written within the clay before the tile had been baked; and the characters read thus: *"In the Year of the Hare, in the fourth month, on the seventeenth day, at the Hour of the Serpent, this tile, after serving as a pillow, will be thrown at a rat and broken."* Now the prediction had really been fulfilled at the Hour of the Serpent on the seventeenth day of the fourth month of the Year of the Hare. Greatly astonished, Shoko Setsu once again looked at the fragments, and discovered the seal and the name of the maker. At once he left his hut, and, taking with him the pieces of the tile, hurried to the neighbouring town in search of the tile maker. He found the tile maker in the course of the day, showed him the broken tile, and asked him about its history.

'After having carefully examined the shards, the tile maker said: "This tile was made in my house; but the characters in the clay were written by an old man — a fortune teller — who asked permission to write upon the tile before it was baked." "Do you know where he lives?" asked Shoko Setsu. "He used to live," the tile maker answered, "not very far from here; and I can show you the way to the house. But I do not know his name."

'Having been guided to the house, Shoko Setsu presented himself at the entrance, and asked for permission to speak to the old man. A serving-student courteously invited him to enter, and ushered him into an apartment where several young men were at study. As Shoko Setsu took his seat, all the youths saluted him. Then the one who had first addressed him bowed and said: "We are grieved to inform you that our master died a few days ago. But we have been waiting for you, because he predicted that you would come today at this house, at this very hour. Your name is Shoko Setsu, and our master told us to give you a book which he believed would be of service to you. Here is the book; please to accept it."

'Shoko Setsu was not less delighted than surprised; for the book was a manuscript of the rarest and most precious kind, containing all the secrets of the science of divination. After having thanked the young men, and properly expressed his regret for the death of their teacher, he went back to his hut, and immediately proceeded to test the worth of the book by consulting its pages in regard to his own fortune. The book suggested to him that on the south side of his dwelling, at a particular spot near one corner of the hut, great luck awaited him. He dug at the place indicated, and found a jar containing gold enough to make him a very wealthy man.'

My old acquaintance left this world as lonesomely as he had lived in it. Last winter, while crossing a mountain-range, he was overtaken by a snowstorm, and lost his way. Many days later he was found standing erect at the foot of a pine, with his little pack strapped to his shoulders: a statue of ice — arms folded and eyes closed as in meditation. Probably, while waiting for the storm to pass, he had yielded to the drowsiness of cold, and the drift had risen over him as he slept. Hearing of this strange death I remembered the old Japanese saying, *Uranaiya minouye shiradzu:* 'The fortune teller knows not his own fate.'[9]

10
Life's Unluckiest Hour

'Fates, we would know your pleasures;
That we shall die, we know.'
                    — William Shakespeare, *Julius Caesar*

If the fortune teller knows not his own fate, then what of the rest of us? Judging from ancient and modern tradition, it appears that the moment of death *can* be predicted, although it cannot always be averted, and sometimes it is not even advisable to try.

In Imperial Rome, to foretell the death of the emperor was punishable by the death of the foreteller, and similar penalties have been assessed in more modern times for similar offences.

Mother Shipton is surely the most famous of all English psychics, and she nearly lost her life for foretelling the death of Cardinal Wolsey. There were rumours abroad that she had predicted the Cardinal would never see York, and that was generally taken to mean that he would not *live* to see York. Mother Shipton had already acquired quite a reputation as psychic, and her predictions were taken quite seriously.

News of the prophecy eventually reached the Cardinal himself, and he sent the Duke of Suffolk and Lords Piercy and Darcy to pay the old lady a visit. As soon as they arrived she gave them what they interpreted to be unmistakable evidence of her psychic gifts, for she was able to call all of them by their correct names and titles, even though she had never seen any of them before. As for the prophecy, though, she insisted that the rumours were not quite right. The Cardinal would *see* York, she said; he just wouldn't *arrive* there. She admitted that she was predicting his death, however, and that was apparently what everyone was worried about. The Duke threatened to have her burned at the stake for even suggesting such a thing, but the seeress was unperturbed. She threw her handkerchief into the fireplace and told him that if *it* burned, so would she. When the handkerchief remained untouched, the lords were greatly moved, and the Duke asked the pythoness what would be *his* fate. She said: 'My lord, the time will come when you shall be as low as I, and that is low indeed.' All of these things happened, just as she had foreseen them.[1]

Josephus tells a similar story about Judas the Essene, a prophet in ancient Palestine who 'never missed the truth in his predictions.' The Essenes actually cultivated and taught the art of predicting the future. In fact, one of their sayings was that 'Fate is the mistress of all things,' and this Judas had a small school of disciples who followed him about in the hope of learning something of these mystic arts. Now Judas had predicted the death of one Antigonus, which was a fairly safe prediction, since the Queen, among others, intended to dispose of him. But the prediction was not at all trivial, since Judas had predicted not only the man's death, but the date on which it would take place. Moreover, he predicted that it would happen in a place called Strato's Tower.

When the day came, Judas saw Antigonus walking about close to the Temple. Strato's Tower was six hundred furlongs from the Temple, and the day was already four hours old. It seemed impossible that the prediction could be fulfilled, and Judas, who apparently was far more concerned for his own reputation as a prophet than for the other man's life, was greatly saddened thereby. Some excellent news came shortly which cheered him up, though. It happened that there were *two* places called Strato's Tower, and one of them, which Josephus describes as 'a subterraneous place', was close by. Antigonus had been summoned to this place by his own brother, and was ambushed in the darkness by his brother's thugs and murdered.[2]

According to Carleton, Paulus Tertius warned his son of his approaching death, with what we might call deadly accuracy,[3] and Cicero says that just before he was condemned, Socrates called his disciple Cebes into his cell and told him the verdict would be unfavourable. He had, he said, had a dream, in which appeared a young woman of extraordinary beauty who quoted this verse from Homer: 'Gladly on Pythia's shore the third day's dawn shall behold thee.' It was precisely on the third day that Socrates was condemned and forced to take his own life, by drinking hemlock.[4]

In 1895, W.T. Stead, the publisher of *The Borderland Review*, wrote a letter to the famous British psychic researcher F.W.H. Myers in which he described a premonition from one of his relatives. It seemed that Stead had been planning to take a sea voyage, and the relative believed that the ship he was to board — *The Majestic* — would meet with some kind of disaster. It did not, but the prophecies continued, nonetheless.

In 1897 Stead published a prophecy by a palmist that he would die at the age of 63. As the fateful year approached, he consulted another palmist, the famous Cheiro, and was told that if he happened to be travelling by water in the middle of April, 1912, he would be in danger. Another psychic told him of a dream in which people were somehow struggling at sea. He felt that the dream concerned itself in some way with Stead. Ignoring all these warnings, Stead put out to sea in April of 1912. The captain was the former captain of *The Majestic*, and the ship was *The Titanic*.[5]

The ancients were full of stories like this. Cyrus the Great is said by Cicero to have dreamed that the sun was at his feet. He tried three times to grasp it, and on the third try it disappeared. The soothsayers interpreted the dream to mean that he would reign three decades, and then die at age seventy, which prophecy was fulfilled.[6]

When Callenus of India ascended his funeral pyre he turned to Alexander and said, 'I shall see you very soon,' meaning, presumably, that they would meet in the next world. Alexander died a few days later in Babylon.[7]

In his *Lives of Eminent Philosophers*, Diogenes Laertius tells a story of this nature about the Pythagorean philosopher Pherecydes.

Pherecydes was a personal student of Pythagoras, and a gifted prophet, who was reputed to have frequently foretold future events with uncanny accuracy. Once as he was walking along the beach in Samos he is said to have spied a ship in the distance. He predicted that it would sink, 'and even as he watched her, down she went.' On another occasion he is said to have predicted an earthquake, which occurred on schedule, and the successful siege of Messene, which happened just as he had predicted it.

Hence, when it came time for Pherecydes to die, it would be surprising had he not predicted that as well. According to Hermippus, 'on the eve of war between Ephesus and Magnesia' he told someone: 'Drag me by the legs and place me in the territory of Magnesia; and take a message to your countrymen that after their victory they must bury me there.' The strange message was delivered, and after Ephesus had successfully defeated the Magnesians — again, just as Pherecydes had predicted — 'they found Pherecydes dead and buried him on the spot with great honours.'[8]

Aristotle reports that his friend Eudemus the Cyprian became very ill while passing through the city of Pherae on his way to Macedonia. In a dream he saw a beautiful youth, who told him that he would recover and that the tyrant Alexander, who ruled the city, would die. The dream said furthermore that Eudemus would 'go back home' five years later. The first part of the dream was fulfilled, just as the youth had said, and five years later Eudemus 'went home' in a sense. He died trying to get back to Cyprus from Sicily.[9]

Those who find this story improbable may take comfort from the fact that there is one almost identical to it in Jung's autobiography, *Memories, Dreams, Reflections*. He had a heart attack, and was thought by the hospital staff to be surely close to death, since his body was surrounded by a strange luminescence — one of the common signs of approaching death. After a number of very strange and interesting visions — all of which are described in detail in the book — he was impressed with the fact that it was not 'right' for him to die at that moment, and that he would have to return. His physician, Dr. H., would have to go in his place. On 4 August 1944 Jung was allowed to sit up in his bed for the first time, and on the same day Dr. H. took to his. Dr. H. eventually died of septicemia, and Jung recovered, just as the vision had indicated.[10]

'The daughter of Polycrates dreamed that Jupiter bathed her father, and Apollo anointed him,' says Bacon in his essay 'On Prophecies', 'and it came to pass that he was crucified in an open place, where the Sun [Apollo] made his body run with sweat, and the rain washed it . . . When I was in France, I heard from Dr Penal, that the Queen Mother, who was given to curious arts, caused the King her husband's nativity to be calculated, under a false name; and the astrologer gave a judgement, that he should be killed in a duel; at which the Queen laughed, thinking her husband to be above challenges and duels. But he was slain upon a course at tilt, the splinters of the staff of Montgomery going in at his beaver.'[11] Carleton has this same story in his *Madness of Astrologers*, where we read that the astrologer was one Gauricius, and that he 'warned Henry II of France not to run at Tilt in the 41st year of his Age, for that the Starres did then threaten a wound in his head.'[12]

In the early part of his life, the poet William Cowper met an old lady, who happened to be a fortune teller, and who successfully predicted many of the events which befell him and his family. Now one of the things she said was, that when he should see her again, his death would not be far off. He was not sure whether he saw her for the first time near his father's house at Hertfordshire or elsewhere, but of the second occasion there was no doubt. It was on the walks behind St John's College garden in the year 1770. Shortly thereafter, he became fatally ill and died.[13]

Lord Byron was once accused of plagiarism because he wrote of a white bird hovering over a death-bed in *Don Juan*. But this is hardly fair, because this belief — that white birds portend death — was once a common one in England and still survives in rural areas.

Howell says that he once saw an inscription on a 'huge marble' in a stone cutter's shop in Fleet Street, near St Dunstan's Church, which mentioned this very belief. The first inscription was for John Oxenham, who was described as 'a goodly young man'. According to the tomsbtone, 'as he was struggling with the pangs of death, a bird with a white breast was seen [in his chamber] fluttering about his bed, and so vanished.' This would have been enough to excite a superstitious peasant, but there was more. A second inscription on the same tombstone was for 'Mary Oxenham, sister of the above John.' It says that she 'died the next day' and that '*the same apparition*,' meaning the white bird, '*was in the room*.' Even that is not all, because there was a *third* inscription, for John's son James. According to the stone, James 'died a child in his cradle . . . *and such a bird was seen fluttering about his head a little before he expired*.' It, too, vanished.[14]

The white bird of death also played a part in the story of Lord

Lyttleton's ghost. This story was very well known during the eighteenth and early nineteenth centuries, and is mentioned by Lord Byron among others, but I have not seen any reference to it in modern works, so it may be worthwhile to quote it here. The following comes from the *Memoirs* of Sir Nathaniel Wraxall, Baronet, as published at London in 1815:

He says of Lord Lyttleton that he was:

> a man of very considerable parliamentary abilities, who, notwithstanding the many glaring vices of his private character, might have made a conspicuous political figure, if he had not been carried off in the prime of life.
>
> His father, the first Lord Lyttleton, well known as an Historian, and as a Poet, derived not less respect from the elevation of his mind, and his many domestic virtues. The second Lord Lyttleton, by the profligacy of his conduct, and the abuse of his talents, seemed to emulate Dryden's Duke of Buckingham, or Pope's Duke of Wharton; both of whom he resembled in the superiority of his natural endowments, as well as in the peculiarity of his end. Villiers, the 'Zimri' of Dryden's Poem of 'Absalom and Achitophel,' after exhausting his health, and squandering his immense fortune in every species of excess or riot, expired, as is well known, at a wretched tenement, on his own estate near Helmsley, in Yorkshire, abandoned by all his former admirers. Wharton, who acted a part under George the First, hardly less distinguished or eccentric, than Villiers had performed under Charles the Second; terminated his equally extraordinary career, exiled and attainted, among the Pyrenees, in an obscure monastery of Catalonia, worn out by his pursuit of pleasures. Lyttleton, when scarcely thirty-six, breathed his last at a country house near Epsom, called Pit Place, from its situation in a chalk pit, where he witnessed, as he conceived, a supernatural apprearance.
>
> Having gone down there for purposes of recreation, with a gay party of both sexes, several among whom I personally knew; he had retired to bed when a noise which resembled the fluttering of a bird or pidgeon heard at his chamber window, attracted his attention. He then saw, or thought he saw, a female figure, which approached the foot of the bed, announced to him that in three days precisely from that time, he should be called from this state of existence. In whatever manner the supposed intimation was conveyed, whether by sound or by impression, it is certain that Lord Lyttleton considered the circumstance as real; that he mentioned it as such to those persons who were in the house with him, that it deeply affected his mind, and that he died on the third night, at the predicted hour.

About four years afterward, in the year 1783, dining at Pit Place, I had the curiosity to visit the bed chamber, where the casement window at which, as Lord Lyttleton asserted, the dove appeared to flutter, was pointed out to me. And at his step-mother's, the Dowager Lady Lyttleton's in Portugal-Street, Grosvenor Square, who being a woman of very lively imagination, lent an implicit faith to all the supernatural facts which were supposed to have accompanied or produced Lord Lyttleton's end; I have frequently seen a painting, which she herself executed in 1780, expressly to commemorate the event. It hung in a conspicuous part of her drawing room. There, the dove appears at the window, while a female figure, habited in white, stands at the bed foot, announcing to Lord Lyttleton his dissolution. Every part of the figure was faithfully designed after the description given her by the Valet de Chambre who attended him, to whom his master related all the circumstances. This man assured Lady Lyttleton, that on the night indicated, Lord Lyttleton, who notwithstanding his endeavours to surmount the impression, had suffered under great depression of spirits during the three preceding days, returned to bed before twelve o'clock. Having ordered the Valet to mix him some Rhubarb, he sat up in the bed, apparently in health, intending to swallow the medicine; but being in want of a tea spoon, which the servant had neglected to bring, his master, with a strong expression of impatience, sent him to bring a spoon. He was not absent from the room more than the space of a minute; but when he returned, Lord Lyttleton, who had fallen back, lay motionless in that attitude. No efforts to restore animation were attended with success. Whether, therefore, his death was occasioned by some new shock upon his nerves, or happened in consequence of an Apoplectic or other seizure, must remain a matter of uncertainty and conjecture.

It is however to be observed that the Lyttleton family, either from constitutional nervous irritability, or from other causes, was particularly susceptible of impressions similar to the shock which seems to have produced Lord Lyttleton's end. His father, though a man of very distinguished talent, manifested great credulity, as I have been assured, on the subject of Apparitions; and his cousin, Miss Lyttleton, who married the present Sir Richard Hoare, died in a way somewhat similar, about four years later, at Stourhead. The second Lord Lyttleton's life had likewise been of a nature and description so licentious, not to say abandoned, as to subject him continually to the keenest reproaches of an accusing conscience. This domestic spectre, which accompanied him everywhere, was known to have given rise, while on his travels, particularly at Lyons, to scenes greatly resembling his last moments. Among the females who had been

the objects and the victims of his temporary attachment, was a
Mrs Dawson, whose fortune, as well as her honour and reputation,
fell a sacrifice to her passion. Being forsaken by him, she did not
long survive; and distress of mind was known to have accelerated,
if not to have produced her death. It was her image which haunted
his pillow, and was supposed by him to have announced his
approaching dissolution at Pit Place. [15]

Lord Byron interprets this to mean that 'the souls of the dead'
are believed to '*inhabit* the form of birds'. In illustration of this,
he refers us to the Duchess of Kendall, who believed that she
was visited in this manner by the shade of George I, flying in
her window in the form of a raven. [16] This was was undoubtedly
the inspiration for the famous poem by Edgar Allen Poe, in which
a raven played a similar role, representing the shade of his recently
deceased wife.

In Germany the birds must be a flock of chattering magpies,
and they must alight upon the house of the doomed person. [17]
Jung tells of one of his patients who was a fervent believer in
this regard. His grandmother had died many years before, and
both he and his family had been greatly impressed by the fact
that just as she was about to expire a flock of birds appeared
at her bedroom window. The same thing happened when the
man's mother died, and that convinced him that these stories
about birds and death were not old wives' tales, but actual facts.

The fellow was in his fifties, and after the 'neurosis' that led
him to Jung in the first place cleared up, he developed symptoms
of heart disease. He went to a physician, received a favourable
prognosis, and collapsed in the street and died on the way home
with the medical report in his pocket. According to his wife, earlier
that morning as he left his house for the doctor's office a flock
of birds had alighted upon the roof. [18]

Now death happens to be a primal experience, and Jung
believed that primal experiences gave rise to what he called
'archetypal' phenomena — situations which rise out of the
collective unconscious, and manifest themselves not only in
dreams, but in our daily lives.

In illustration of this, he pointed to the story of the Greek poet
Ibycus. Ibycus was murdered by robbers, and the poet's death
was presaged by a flock of cranes who descended on the scene
of the crime as he was about to expire. This greatly impressed

the robbers, and when another flock of cranes descended to where *they* were standing some time later they were moved to cry out, whereupon they were brought to justice.[19]

One fascinating aspect of these kinds of premonitions is that the efforts one takes to avoid the predicted event frequently help to bring about its fulfilment.

King Croesus had a dream that his son Atys would die by an iron spear point. He woke up in terror, convinced that the dream was prophetic, and resolved to take every precaution to prevent its fulfilment. Atys was not allowed to go to war, and every javelin was kept out of his way, lest some accident occur.

Now it happened that a wild boar wandered into the realm, and since these animals were quite dangerous, the people decided to hunt and kill it. They requested the assistance of Atys, who thought there could surely be no harm, since his father's dream had to do with a *spear* wound not a *tusk* wound. But the hunters carried spears, and an accident occurred in which Atys was fatally wounded, thus fulfilling the prophecy.[20]

I had a rather odd experience like this myself. when I was a child I belonged to an organization which was planning a trip to the beach, several hundred miles from where I was living. The night before the trip was to start, I had a strange dream, in which I was in the cockpit of an aircraft, taking off from the street in front of my house. Just as the plane left the ground, the pilot lost consciousness, and, although I tried to bring it down safely, the plane spun out of control and crashed. Now all dreams are rather odd, but this one bothered me all the next day. I had never been in an aeroplane in my life, and the trip, which I had not planned to go on anyway, was to be *by road*.. Hence, it was difficult to see how the dream could have any significance. Nonetheless a sense of foreboding stayed with me.

I was persuaded to go on the trip anyway, and after I arrived at the rendezvous, it transpired that there had been a change of plans. One of the organizers of the trip was a Naval officer, and he had arranged for us to ride to the beach in a naval aircraft instead of by car. Need I add that the plane developed engine trouble in flight?

This experience left me with a new respect for dreams, particularly if they had anything to do with aeroplanes, and in 1975 it was still on my mind. I was planning a trip to San Francisco, and confided to a friend that with my luck the plane would probably crash in flight over the desert. He told me not to say things like that, because *the night before* he had had a terrible dream about a plane crash! Later that day, two aircraft in another city collided in mid-air in what was at that time the worst air disaster in history. I told myself that his dream had been thus fulfilled, but it was difficult to shake a feeling that this, too, may have been intended as a warning.

Now my flight was scheduled for the following day, and with an acute sense of behaving in a highly foolish manner, I called the airline at the last moment to change flights. When I arrived at the airport, I had a vague sense of having somehow cheated the hangman, mingled with a less pleasant sense of having given in to a private superstition. However, when the hour of departure arrived, we were notified that our flight had been detained. By pure chance, at the last moment, the aircraft mechanics had discovered a problem in one of the engines which, had it not been discovered, would have resulted in a fatal crash. The flight I had *originally* been scheduled for went off without a hitch.

It sometimes works just the opposite way. J.P. Morgan was scheduled to sail on the maiden voyage of the *Titanic*, but was seized at the last moment by some urge to cancel his reservation. [21]

According to another story which comes from Cicero, Simonides is said to have discovered the exposed body of a dead man and to have taken the time to bury it, thereby winning the gratitude of the dead man's shade. Some time afterward he was about to take a sea voyage and saw the man in a dream, warning him not to go. He heeded the dead man's warning and thereby saved his own life. All those who went perished in a shipwreck. [22]

Jerome Cardan, whom we met in a previous chapter, is said to have predicted his own death twice. He outlived the first date he predicted, then re-calculated, and died right on schedule. The neatness of that coincidence moved some of his critics to suspect suicide, which prompted Eliphas Levi, with tongue in cheek, to pronouce Cardan 'a martyr to his own faith in astrology.' [23] But if we accept the theories of certain occultists, that may not be entirely fair. Even though the first prediction did not come true, it may have been accurate, nonetheless, and here we connect with luck.

Madam Blavatsky says that 'for every man there is a [climacteric],' which is a moment in his life 'when he must draw near to death.' She does not say *why* these climacterics should exist, but she does suggest that they are preordained in some way, and that they are survivable with luck and skill. If the person encountering the climacteric 'has squandered his life-powers,' she says, 'there is no escape for him, but if he has lived according to the law, he may pass through and so continue in the same body almost indefinitely.' She says that this is the explanation for the alchemists' Elixir of Immortality, which she says is 'no fable', but 'only the veil hiding a real occult process, warding off age and dissolution for periods which would seem fabulous' to the uninitiated.[24] If this is true, Cardan could have survived one climacteric and been caught by another.

In *The Wisdom of the Mystic Masters*, Joseph Weed calls these times 'death points', and he says that most of us have several. He mentions a lady in New York, who was 'told' psychically that her son would have two of these spaced fifteen years apart. Now the first of these was to take place in Europe just before he reached his twenty-second birthday, but his family lived in New York and had no intention of visiting Europe, so they thought nothing of it. As it does, fate started taking some of its strange twists, and the son found himself in Europe anyway, and just at the time prophesied. Hitler had declared war on the USA, the son enrolled in Officers Candidate School, and was sent to France. Two days before his twenty-second birthday he was shot and killed by a sniper's bullet.[25]

In some cases, the climacteric seems impossible to stop. On 21 February 1928, according to a copyrighted story in *The New York Times*,

an extraordinary drama of incompetence or indifference on the part of officials and employees of a sanatorium came before a court at Amiens . . . in a trial in which six persons were found guilty of the accidental death of M Desnoyelles, an inmate of the sanatorium.

The defendants were Dr Carriat, the chief physician; Drs Sturbini and Simon, internes; M Saune, the pharmacist; Mlle Lecomte, his assistant; and Superintendent Helleu.

According to the evidence, Mr Desnoyelles died from a potion administered to him by Dr Simon, the interne, but investigation showed a strange list of errors which resulted in this poisonous concoction being offered to this particular patient.

The chief physician made the prescription for another patient, M Desmalles, who was suffering from sciatica. But he neglected to check the prescription to see that it had been written down as he had ordered.

The interne Sturbini, who filled out the prescription, confused two drugs, introducing one of a poisonous nature. Then, in addition, he wrote down the order on a slip used for prescriptions for internal use instead of on a slip for prescriptions for external use.

The pharmacist, who was busy at the time, gave the prescription to his assistant to fill, and she did not check it. Mlle Lecomte filled the prescription as indicated, except that she made a mistake in the name of the patient, inscribing it with the name of M Desnoyelles instead of that of M Desmalles.

To complete the list of almost unbelievable errors, the interne Simon, according to the testimony, instead of administering the medicine according to the dose prescribed, handed the patient the bottle and told him to 'take a good big drink.'[26]

Even the ancient disciples of the medieval mystic C.R.C. could not ward off their climacterics for ever, at least not if we believe their biographer. He says that despite all their formidable occult powers, and 'although they were free from all diseases and pain, yet, notwithstanding, they could not live and pass their time appointed of God.' They claimed that they couldn't even *foresee* their deaths, because 'although before our eyes we behold the image and pattern of all the world, yet . . . our misfortunes, [and] hour of death [are] only known to God Himself, who thereby would have us keep in a continual readiness.' But the writer nonetheless insisted that 'Brother C.' foretold the death of Brother I.O., the first of the Fraternity to die, long before it happened.[27] What are we to make of all this?

Well, we are not without theories, and to silence my critics beforehand, let me emphasize that I am not representing these as anything more than theories. As usual, the most advanced speculations — to my mind, anyway — come from the Far East, from the yogis of India and Tibet.

The yogis maintain that each of us is karmically allotted so many breaths, and that when our allotted number of breaths is up, *our* number is up as well.

This is one of the theories underlying the practice of *pranayama*, or yogic breathing. Long before science ever discovered the importance of stress in hastening one's final departure, and long before stress was shown to be measurable in terms of one's breathing, the yogis figured out that by slowing down one's breathing, one could in effect extend one's life. In theory if you could learn to breathe only half as many times in a minute as you do ordinarily, you should be able to live twice as long. In fact, there are stories of yogic saints living in the high Himalayas who have been with us for centuries, just by keeping their nostrils plugged up and contenting themselves with an occasional snort, rather than the greedy and intemperate gasping most of the rest of us indulge in. Those stories are largely undocumented, of course, but it seems logical that if you really *do* have a specific number of breaths allotted to you, something in you must be keeping score. As your allotted number runs out, your internal scorekeeper might cause some inner movement of the soul, which would be interpreted as a premonition of death.

In the *Yoga Sutras*, Patanjali suggests that advanced yogis may be able to bring on these premonitions voluntarily by performing *Sanyama* on karma. But Vyasa, in his learned commentary on the subject, suggests that this refers to the signs that manifest themselves when death is imminent. He points out, for example, that if you put your fingers in your ears and you cannot hear the noise of vital functions taking place within your body, or you close your eyes and you do not see the 'inner light', or if you suddenly see visions of angels coming to take you away (or demons, if you are headed in the opposite direction), you know that death is very near indeed.[28]

When this happens, there are often signs which may be discerned by others, particularly if they happen to have gifted sight. We have already seen how, when Jung was about to die, his nurses saw a glow around him. In his little pamphlet on *Auras*, Edgar Cayce says that he once saw the auras disappear around a whole lift full of people. He suspected that something was wrong, and immediately afterward the cable holding the lift aloft snapped. Everyone on board was killed.

In his *Miscellanies*, which were published in 1723, John Aubrey has a whole chapter on 'Second Sight', the Scottish name for clairvoyance, along with numerous examples of visions that foretell impending death. If the person in the vision is to be hanged, they will see him with a rope around his neck. If he is to be beheaded, they will see him without a head. If he is to be drowned, they see him with water up to his neck, whereas if the death is to come in some unexpected manner, they will see him with a winding sheet around his head. Aubrey got one of these stories from a 'Highland Gentleman' named MacDonald. He had been visited by his brother, but 'saw' the chap without a head. Naturally, he did not discuss such an extraordinary experience with the brother, but it turned out to be prophetic. The brother happened to be a murderer. Within 24 hours of the vision, he was arrested and beheaded, and his head sent to Edinburgh. Nor did Aubrey consider this story unique. 'Many such Instances could be given,' he said, although considering their nature, we may perhaps be thankful that they were not. [29]

In an essay called 'The Soul and Death', Jung says that he was 'able to follow' the 'unconscious psychic activity' of 'a great many' of his patients 'into the immediate presence of death. The approaching end,' he says, 'was indicated by those symbols which, in normal life also, proclaim changes of psychological condition – rebirth symbols such as change of locality, journeys, and the like', and he says that he was 'frequently . . . able to trace back for over a year, in the dream series, the indications of approaching death.' [30] This would suggest that the Inner Self *knows*, even if the outer man does not, and what is more, according to the Swiss doctor, the Inner Self takes this apocalyptic event very calmly, almost as if it were a mere incident in an evolution that has already continued for millions of years, and which is destined to continue for millions more. In some instances the outer man begins to prepare as it were unconsciously, as if he senses his own approaching doom, and yet does not wish to openly admit that fact.

I have noticed with several persons of my own acquaintance that they came to take a great interest in religious matters a year or so before they were to die, even though religion might have been a low priority item in their lives until that time. In fact, I have often suspected that a spectacular conversion on the part of a person who has been a lifelong unbeliever might be an advance indicator of the soul, in its inscrutable wisdom, preparing for its departure.

11

The Psychology of Luck

There are two kinds of people in the world where luck is concerned – namely, those who are lucky and those who are not – and that being the case, we should not be surprised that there are two kinds of thinking in the world about luck. Those who seem to have plenty of it like to pat themselves on the back for it. Luck to them is not something that just somehow happens. You make your own luck. But to the unlucky it is different. Luck is a stroke from the blue; it is 'the slings and arrows of outrageous fortune.' They do not know where it comes from or why. They only know that it does not seem to come in their direction.

There is considerable merit to both of those approaches, but if we want to be *more* lucky, it makes sense that we might want to emulate those who already *are* more lucky. It may be worthwhile to take personal responsibility for the luck that you have, and consider how you might be able to make it better.

At base, luck has to do with man's two most primitive motivations: money and sex. And if we keep that in mind, it is easy to classify people into just a few luck categories. Figuring out which one of those you fit into may give you some valuable insights into how you create the luck that you do – that part of it that you create, anyway. And it can give you some valuable insights into how to change it – if that is what you decide you want to do.

Now people do not strive for nothing. If we work, we work *for* something, and that 'something' that we work for is our economic motivation. If we classify people according to their economic motivations, we can distinguish four definite Luck Types.

The most basic economic motivation any of us can have is the instinct to survive, and we can say that Luck Type Number One is motivated by just that — he wants to survive.

Now *all* of us want to survive, but Type Number One's motive in working is *primarily* to survive. His values are not necessarily economic in character, and it can be said of him that he works to live, and does not live to work. He tends to consider work a necessary evil which he must endure to meet his goal of survival, and he tends to resent an industrial state which forces him to put out more effort than is logically required to meet his goal. He has excellent insight into his motives and aspirations, and he makes rational choices throughout life which ensure that he gets what he wants. Since his purely economic goals are modest, he tends not to see an advanced education as necessary for their realization, and tends to leave school at an earlier age than Types Number Two or Three. He does not like books or bookish people, and he tends to value hands-on experience over theoretical learning. Politically, Type Number One is part of a large and very well defined constituency in every country where he may be found. Once his goal of survival has been taken care of, his motivation for further effort of a purely economic character tends to evaporate, but he is capable of almost superhuman feats to achieve his basic goal, if it proves difficult. An excellent example of this is the heroic efforts of the Russian peasants to defend their Motherland against German aggression during the Second World War.

Type Number Two wants to survive, just as Type Number One does, but in addition, he wants to enjoy certain luxuries above and beyond the bare necessities. He tends to be educated more extensively than Type Number One, since he has to attain a higher income to achieve his goals, and he has considerably less of what we might call class consciousness, since the Type Number Twos of the world are a much more amorphous group than their Type Number One brethren. This type of person is well represented in the skilled trades and the professions.

Type Number Three wants to survive, just as Type Number One does, and he may want to enjoy some amenities, just as Type Number Two does, but he mainly wants to own and operate something. Whereas Type Number Two may be found in the managerial class, Type Number Three supplies a society with its entrepreneurs and financiers. He may be contemptuous of luxuries, and for that reason sometimes becomes a *miser,* seeking money for its own sake or for the power it brings rather than for the things it can buy. He will work long hours for a lower standard of living than the average Type Number Two enjoys, and yet his income, since it has no upper bound, may be spectacularly large, drawing considerable envy and resentment from his Type Number Two brethren, who do not understand his motivation. He has little use for leisure time, is contemptuous of people he considers 'lazy' and tends to own and operate capitalist societies for his own benefit.

He is easily distinguished from Type Number One because he works much longer hours. And he is easily distinguished from Type Number Two because Type Number Two never gets into any serious capital formation. He works so he can quickly enjoy the fruits of his labour, and he often says of himself that he spends everything he makes. Type Number Two tends to think of that situation as somehow inevitable, but Type Number Three makes sacrifices to accumulate riches, and the Type Number Threes of the world tend to *own* the world, except in societies where private ownership is prohibited by the government. Whereas Type Number Two works so that he may indulge in pleasures, to Type Number Three work *is* pleasure. He therefore tends to work all his life, whereas Types Number One and Two yearn for retirement. Since he controls the assets whereby the other types realize their economic goals, he sets the rules, at least in capitalist societies, and tends to be the most bitterly resented of all the three.

In addition we can posit the existence of a Type Number Four, whose economic motivation is that he *has* no economic motivation. In their negative aspect, Type Number Fours may be found among the derelicts and refuse of the world, but this type is not *necessarily* negative by any means. The mere fact that someone's motivation is not economic in character does not mean that it does not exist, and in the positive aspect Type Number Four may be found among the selfless of the world, who, needing and desiring nothing for themselves, live only to serve others. As a practical matter, this type of person will be found mainly among those religious orders which have a humanitarian mission to fulfil, but they need no words from me on how to be lucky.

Whole societies tend to be dominated by one or another of these types, and in fact it appears that one of the goals of these different groups is to achieve the dominant position in society. Yet the members of these different groups do not understand each other's needs and motivations, and they typically regard each other with both disdain and suspicion.

When Type Number Three dominates a society, we have classical, *laissez faire* capitalism. Hong Kong is the purest example of this, although the Red Chinese can be expected to put a stop to that in 1997. There is much dynamism, fortunes are made and lost easily, and envy is kept from becoming a destructive force by the general perception that anyone can 'make it'. Those who are low today may be high tomorrow, and although this is certainly a myth in most cases, it is a myth that seems to work surprisingly well. In any event, this type of society seems to be characteristic only of industrial states which have started their industrial development recently, and which therefore enjoy rates of economic growth which are the envy of their more mature neighbours.

Once an industrial society acquires a certain maturity, it also acquires a certain middle class, which is to say people who own and operate nothing, but who live very well. These people come into their own politically in due course, and then we have what is contemptuously described in certain quarters as a *bourgeois* society. The long hours of poorly rewarded labour which are still such a scourge in Asia, and even Japan, are replaced by the forty hour week and high wages. Industrial growth slows down, concern for quality of life takes precedence over concern for economic growth, and the order of the day is how to balance the universal desire for a high standard of living with the need for ample time to enjoy it. Society, in short, comes to reflect the attitudes and values of its Type Number Two citizens. These countries are the most pleasant places in the world in which to live, but they all share one fatal and tragic flaw which is a natural result of their emphasis on consuming rather than accumulating wealth: they are all in economic decline.

In some instances, usually after some kind of military action, a society comes to be dominated by Type Number One. Many of the so-called 'communist' states fall in this category, and they reflect the values of Type Number One, which are that luxury is not so greatly important, and that man should work for survival. Since survival can be interpreted to mean military strength, some of these societies are very strong militarily, and place tremendous emphasis on military readiness, but most of them are not self-indulgent in the sense that the middle-class states are. For this reason their people tend to live at the survival level, and they are sometimes condemned as economic 'failures' by the people who run Type Number Two societies. This is hardly fair, though, because the Type Number One states which are truly independent tend to be quite successful, according to their own modes of reckoning. They have established the supremacy of Type Number One over the other three types, and they have made his values those of the society as a whole.

Since Type Number One seems to have a much greater sense of what we call class consciousness than members of other groups, these societies tend also to be less tolerant of the suppressed classes, and particularly the hated entrepreneurs who make up Type Number Three. The Soviet Union is definitely a Type Number One society, and although 'no accurate figures are available,' the editors of *The Economist* reckon 'that some 400 successful businessmen' in that country 'are still disposed of each year by shooting.'[1] Type Number Two is also suppressed, although with less vigour, and there is some suppression of Type Number Four, which takes the form of laws against malingering, and certain types of religious persecution. The Type Number One personality, who is inaccurately referred to as the 'the working class', tends to be glorified, which is only natural, and there tends to be some overt hostility to learning, although this varies considerably from one country to the next. A typical example of this is the Lysenko affair in Stalin's Russia, or the anti-intellectual campaigns waged by Adolf Hitler. Hitler especially is said to have boasted that he never read a book in his life, and never allowed himself to be photographed with a book nearby. He also 'reformed' his country's educational system along anti-intellectual lines, with results that were not to the liking of some of his countrymen. All of these phenomena are just the logical results of the premises on which Type Number One societies are founded, and the same thing is true of societies dominated by the other types.

All of these types are 'lucky' in their own way. If you are Type Number Two there is no reason to believe that Type Number

Three is luckier than you are, or that any of these orientations is in any way superior to yours. Each of them has its own attractions and demands, and each is particularly suitable to different kinds of personalities. The only thing that matters is whether the *kind* of luck you are creating for yourself is the kind you really want.

Many people have difficulty making up their minds, and this is one of several things that can lead to a distinctly *un*-lucky lifestyle. It is one of the causes of what psychologists call the 'Fear of Success' syndrome.

The 'Fear of Success' syndrome was first noticed by Sigmund Freud, the father of psychoanalysis, and it puzzled him considerably, because psychoanalytic theory holds that nervous difficulties are caused by *frustration*, and not gratification. Nonetheless, Freud says that 'people occasionally fall ill precisely when a deeply-rooted and long-cherished wish has come to fulfilment. It seems as though they were not able to tolerate their happiness; for there can be no question that there is a causal connection between their success and their falling ill.'[2]

An example of this is a young girl who ran from home and 'roved about the world in search of adventures.' In time, she met an artist, moved in with him, and lived with him for many years.

In due course, the artist asked her to marry him, and the girl, in Freud's words, 'began to go to pieces.' She neglected her housekeeping, became suspicious of her would-be husband's relatives and friends, tried to obstruct his artistic work, and eventually succumbed to mental illness.

In another instance, a teacher was offered a promotion, and not *just* a promotion, but a promotion that he had coveted for many years. His own original teacher had retired, and he had been asked to fill the older man's position. Yet instead of giving him happiness, this success plunged him into the depths of depression, and left him 'unfitted for all activity for some years.'[3]

This kind of thing is more common than one might think, and it is one of the principal reasons why many people are not more lucky than they are.

One of the reasons for it, as I said, is that it is just difficult to make up one's mind which of the available lifestyles one wants to pursue. If you pursue an advanced education, you have to give up the leisure and pleasures that could be yours if you took life easier. But then again, if you succeed in acquiring that education, there may be advantages later. If you start your own business, you have to give up the affluence and leisure that you could have as an employee, and you have to face the real possibility that the business could fail, and saddle you with debts for years to come. Then again, if you do *not* start your own business, you will never be your own master. You must work when someone else tells you to, for whatever he wants to pay, doing whatever he wants you to do. It is easy to see how you may be drawn toward independence while working for someone else, and drawn toward working for someone else when contemplating independence. These are tough decisions to make, and people sometimes find themselves vacillating — going first in one direction, then another, never getting anywhere, and wondering why their 'luck' is so bad.

Having known quite a lot of small businessmen personally, I am convinced that this is the principal reason for the high failure rate. It is not possible to be a successful Type Number Three unless you basically give up the Type Number Two lifestyle — and yet they are both so good to pursue.

Other people fear they will not have enough time to pursue their hobbies and interests if they are too lucky. Women sometimes tend to feel that success and femininity do not go together. And they are frequently encouraged in this belief by male competitors. Still another cause of ill luck is a submerged feeling that maybe one really cannot make it after all. If this type of person does not try very hard, or unconsciously defeats himself in various ways, he *knows* why he is unlucky — at least at some level of awareness. It is certainly not that he lacks talent. But if he gives it everything he has and *then* fails he could find that devastating. Some people set themselves up to fail in order to avoid that experience.

Another cause of the Fear of Success syndrome is guilt. Luck is a relative thing. Being lucky or unlucky means being *more* lucky or *more* unlucky than others. And if you are more lucky than other people are, you can expect some envy and resentment to come your way. You can expect to make enemies of people whom you have done no wrong, and you can expect to reap malice from surprising and unexpected quarters. This makes some people feel guilty, and they recoil from luck and success in order to appease their less successful brethren.

Freud believed that this feeling of guilt was 'closely connected to the Oedipus complex . . . as perhaps, indeed, is our feeling of guilt in general.'[4] But I suspect there is a different reason.

In order to make society a viable institution, children are taught to try to make their actions pleasing to others, and nobody could quarrel with this. Courtesy, and consideration for others' feelings are essential to civilized living. But this striving can take on some more questionable aspects as well. Conformity is a way of striving to please others, too. And failure is another. Many people will be 'pleased' if you fail, who may not be so pleased if you succeed. The social signals which they send you may affect your behaviour in subtle ways, perhaps even without you being aware of it. If 'pleasing' other people is important to you, you may find that failure is the price you have to pay.

This may be one of the reasons why there are so many prickly characters in high places in the business world. It may be that for the reasons mentioned, great success often goes to the person who practically revels in other people's envy and resentment. It is almost as if these folks have their responses turned around backward from the rest of us. Whereas resentful signals discourage others who are equally talented but less successful, it may be that they spur the successful on.

These resentful signals are particularly difficult to work around when they come from your parents. A recent study at a major university suggests that as many as eighty per cent of all the people in the industrialized world never make it out of the economic class into which they were born. Every parent wants his child to do well — but not *too* well. Ideally, he should do about as well as mother and father. I know a fellow personally who has acquired a Master's Degree in electrical engineering and who has yet to spend a single day on the job as an engineer. His parents were immensely proud of him for completing an advanced education, since he was the very first person in his family ever to do so. But at the same time they made it quite clear to him that if he wanted to be part of the family, he would do well to pursue the skilled trades, just as his father had done, and his father's father, and his father before him.

Still another source of success guilt is the inevitable conflict between competitive behaviour and what most of us consider acceptable moral values. War is the ultimate competitive activity, and it clearly involves immoral behaviours, but the same thing is true of competition at less intense levels.

Jealousy, envy, egotism, and selfishness are essentially competitive behaviours, and have their origin psychologically in the belief that we should all be in competition with each other. Yet most people recognize these behaviours (in others, at any rate), as at least *non*-moral, if not positively *im*-moral behaviours. These kinds of behaviours are discouraged in children during childhood, and yet the competitive spirit which gives rise to them is encouraged. This produces strong ambivalent feelings in most people where competition is concerned, and those feelings are sometimes very difficult to resolve.

Some people solve the problem by reconciling morality and competition in ways which are ingenious but logically outrageous. Vengeance seeking, which is a competitive activity, becomes 'morally justified' by the injury which provoked it. The victim has a 'right' to his pound of flesh. Sexual jealousy becomes righteous indignation. Xenophobia becomes an admirable manifestation of patriotism and national pride. This works after a fashion, but it is not completely satisfactory.

Other people try to solve the problem by discouraging competitive behaviours altogether. This approach has considerably more merit to it in my judgement. Women in particular tend toward this solution, and it is the theoretical basis of at least one variety of socialism. But there are some problems with this approach as well, at least as it has been historically implemented.

The difficulty is that many people see competition as necessarily tied in with excellence. People who argue in favour of the competitive society maintain that excellence can only be achieved if people are in competition with each other. Hence, those who believe that the evils which result from an excess of competitiveness should be reduced or eliminated tend to aim at reducing excellence itself. The ideal is to reduce everyone and everything to the lowest common denominator.

It is impossible for anyone to argue against the underlying motive, but this way of approaching the problem sometimes leads to absurdities. Farmers are paid not to plant, workers are paid not to work, union leaders are paid not to strike, and corporations are paid not to show a profit. In some particularly advanced countries professors are paid not to think, students are paid not to learn, and soldiers are paid not to fight. We all know that some bureaucrats are paid not to do anything at all, and that the same thing holds true in some instances for elected officials. It is difficult to escape the feeling that rather than bring in the millennium, this sort of thing merely encourages cynicism.

There are other possibilities, though. Rather than do away with excellence, you can strive for excellence for its own sake, and not to competitively crush someone else, or deprive him of the fruits of attainment. Achievement in any form will be resented by a few, because some people will interpret it in competitive terms. But if you strive for excellence just for its own sake there is no reason why you should feel *guilty*, and it is the *guilt*, and the subtle effects that guilt has on your luck that is the issue, not someone else's resentment.

Another possibility is to pursue success competitively, but with the same 'morality' that applies on the tennis court or the soccer field. Rather than seeing competition as War, and competitors as The Enemy, you can look at the whole thing as a game, to be played by certain implicit rules, and without ill will towards your fellow players. We would all think ill of a tennis player who threw his games in the name of equality, or who tried to physically attack his opponent. However, if he plays according to the generally accepted rules of sportsmanship, we do not see any 'moral' crisis at all. He may be competing very vigorously, but without malice, hatred, jealousy, and all the other vile emotions that competitive types sometimes display outside the sporting environment.

Another unconscious process that sometimes produces bad luck is what we might call the 'break-even mentality'. This kind of person is likely to say that he really does not want to get *ahead*; he just wants to keep from losing what he has. This type of person is very often seen in the investment world. He does not want to make any money out of his investments, actually; he just wants to play the game for awhile and get out without losing anything. Unfortunately, things do not work that way, and he tends to get out after losing *everything*.

Browning had this one all wrong. A man's reach *will* exceed his grasp, and the way to keep from losing what you have may be to strive to get more. If you are only partially successful in getting ahead, that may translate into complete success in standing your ground. Partial success in keeping what you have, on the other hand, could translate into total failure.

Another problem that arises from such things as the break-even mentality is that these things are difficult to keep in water-tight compartments. They tend to ripple and wave throughout your life, and a desire to 'break even' in the business world or in investments or socially but to do well everywhere else *could* translate into a break-even life. It may be that you have to strive to do well in *all* areas of your life in order to keep from unconsciously breaking even in all of them.

And then there are some of the bits of folk wisdom that most of us have been taught from an early age. We all know, for example, that money does not buy happiness – but what does? Does poverty buy happiness? Have you ever asked a poor person that question?

Most of us have an awareness of what kind of luck we are creating at some level, although we may not have as much insight as we might like. Hence, set this book aside and ask yourself honestly: 'Am I creating the kind of luck I want?' If you are, then there is nothing more to do. You are as lucky as anyone could ever hope to be in this lifetime. And if you are not, possibly you might want to do some self-examination. You might find that you want to make some changes here and there – possibly throwing out some of those old attitudes and habits that have kept you back for so long. If you have the time and money, you might want to consider consulting with some of the specialists who make a full-time business of helping people understand how they got to where they are, and how they can get to where they want to go. But whatever you do, best wishes. And good luck.

References

Chapter 1:

1. Arthur Koestler, *Janus*, (Random House, New York, 1978), p. 229.
2. John Toland, *Adolf Hitler*, (Ballantine Books, New York, 1976).
3. 'Dawdling Saved One Man's Life', *New York Times*, 6 January 1967.
4. 'Alton (Illinois) Evening Telegram Obituary Reporter's Vacation Coincides With Unprecendented Week of Unreported Deaths', *New York Times*, 1 September 1946.
5. Harold Helfer, 'Strange to Say', *Fate*, February 1983, p. 76.
6. Camille Flammarion (1842-1925), *L'Inconnu, The Unknown*. (Harper and Brothers, London and New York, 1900. Copyright attributed to Camille Flammarion).
7. *Ibid.*
8. Wilhelm Scholz, *Der Zufall: eine Vorform des Schicksals*. (W. Haedecke, Stuttgart, 1924).
9. Arthur Koestler, 'Mysterious Power of Chance', *The Sunday Times*, 5 May 1974. (*The Times* requested its readers to send in coincidence stories in 1973, and this story was the prize-winning entry.)
10. *Ptolemy's Tetrabiblos, or Quadripartite: Being Four Books of the Influences of the Stars*, translated by J.M. Ashmand. (Davis and Dickson, London, 1822).
11. *Ibid.*, p. 10n.

12. 'Sandburg, at 89, is Taking Life Easy', *The New York Times*, 6 January 1967.

13. Michael Kaufman, 'Pearl Harbour Attack is Linked to Ads', *The New York Times*, 12 March 1967.

14. Arthur Koestler, et al., *The Challenge of Chance, Experiments and Speculations*. (Hutchinson and Co., Ltd., London, 1973).

15. Robert A. Wilson, 'Mere Coincidence?', *Science Digest*, January 1982, pp. 83-85, 95.

16. Martin Gardner, 'Mathematical Games: Why The Long Arm of Coincidence Is Usually Not as Long As It Seems', *Scientific American*, p. 112B.

17. John Gliedman, 'Amazing Numerical Coincidences', *Science Digest*, May 1981, pp. 58-59, 118.

Chapter 2:

1. Quoted by Marc Scot Zicree in *The Twilight Zone Reader*, (Bantam Books, New York, 1982, p. 247).

2. Flammarion, op. cit., p. 198.

3. Jean Francois Steiner, *Treblinka*, translated by Helen Weaver, (Simon and Schuster, New York, 1967).

4. Edmund A. Gehan, 'Note on the "Birthday Problem" ', *The American Statistician*, 16 April, p. 28.

5. Martin Gardner, 'Mathematical Games: Why The Long Arm Of Coincidence Is Usually Not As Long As It Seems', *Scientific American*, p. 110.

6. 'Trials: The Law of Probability', *Time*, 8 January 1965, p. 42.

7. 'Decisions: Trial by Mathematics', *Time*, 26 April 1968, p. 41.

8. Flammarion, op. cit., p. 200n.

9. *Ibid.*, pp. 200-1

10. Martin E. Marty, 'Math and the Messiah', *The Christian Century*, 5 March 1980, p. 271.

11. Francis Bacon, 'On Prophecies', In *Essays, Moral Economical, and Political*, (W. Tegg, London, 1810). This coincidence was originally pointed out by the Roman historians Tacitus and Suetonius.

12. Arthur Koestler, et al., *The Challenge of Chance, Experiments and Speculations*, (Hutchinson and Co., Ltd., London 1973).

13. Stanley Milgram, 'The Small World Problem, *Psychology Today*, May 1967, pp. 66-68.

14.   *Ibid.*
15.   William Manchester, *American Caesar,* (Dell Publishing Company, New York, 1978, p. 32).
16.   Cicero, *De Divinatione,* translated by William A. Falconer, (Wm. Heinemann, London, 1964, XXV, p. 281).
17.   Alan Vaughan, *Incredible Coincidence.* (J.B. Lippincott Co., New York, 1979, p. 206).
18.   Curt Suplee, 'Lotto Baloney', *Harper's* July 1983, pp. 15-16.
19.   Flammarion, op. cit.
20.   Dean Havron, 'Lightning Struck', *Science Digest,* p. 57.
21.   Quoted by Martin Gardner, 'Mathematical Games: Why the Long Arm of Chance Is Usually Not As Long As It Seems', *Scientific American,* p. 110.
22.   *Guinness Book of World Records,* edited and compiled by Norris D. McWhirter, et al., (Bantam Books, New York, 1984, p. 422).
23.   Andrew D. White, *A History of the Warfare of Science With Theology in Christendom,*(D. Appleton, New York, 1898).

Chapter 3:

1.   'Unusual Obits of Past 12 Months', *New York Times,* 10 February 1946.
2.   Quoted by Warren Weaver, *Lady Luck, The Theory of Probability,* (Anchor Books, New York, 1963 p. 281).
3.   Ely Culbertson, *The Strange Lives of One Man.* (John C. Winston & Co., Philadelphia, 1970).
4.   'Dolly Sisters Win $850,000 at Cannes Casino; Its $1,250,000 Losses Heaviest Since 1920', *New York Times,* 29 February 1928.
5.   Flammarion, op. cit.
6.   Weaver, op. cit.
7.   Flammarion, op. cit.
8.   'Gambler's Ruin', *Scientific American,* June 1982, p. 81.
9.   'Critical Values of the Number of Runs', from F. James Rohlf and Robert R. Sokal, *Statistical Tables.* (W.H. Freeman and Co., San Francisco, 1969). The authors claim these tables were copied by them from F.S. Swed and C. Eisenhart's tables in *Ann. Math. Stat.,* 14:66-87, 1943.
10.   Kammerer, *Das Gesetz der Serie,* quoted by Arthur Koestler, *Janus,* p. 261.

11. Kammerer, op. cit., quoted by Arthur Koestler, *The Roots of Coincidence*, (Random House, New York, 1972), p. 84; and *The Case of the Midwife Toad*, (Random House, New York, 1972), p. 137.
12. John Edensor Littlewood, *Mathematician's Miscellany*, (Methuen, London, 1953), pp. 105-106.
13. Koestler, *Challenge of Chance*, pp. 180-185.
14. *Ibid.*
15. Michael Korda, *Success!* (Ballantine Books, New York, 1978), pp. 241-2.
16. Winston Churchill, *The Hinge of Fate*, (Houghton Mifflin, New York, 1950).
17. Arthur Koestler *Janus*, p. 262.

Chapter 4:

1. Mark Twain, *Pudd'nhead Wilson and those Extraordinary Twins*, edited by Sid E. Berger, (Norton, New York, 1980).
2. Quoted by H. Przibram, 'Paul Kammerer als Biologe', in *Monistische Monatshefte*, November, 1926, referenced in Arthur Koestler, *The Roots of Coincidence*, p. 87n.
3. 'Adam Smith' (pseud.), *The Money Game*, (Random House, New York, 1968).
4. 'Why Some Experts Say You Can't Beat the Stock Averages,' *Changing Times*, May 1980.
5. Quoted by 'Adam Smith', op. cit., p. 148.
6. *Ibid.*
7. 'The Dart Board Fund', *Forbes*, 1 October 1973, p. 30.
8. Andrew Tobias, *Still the Only Investment Guide You'll Ever Need*, (Bantam, New York, 1983), p. 105.
9. *Ibid.*
10. 'Most Professionals Lagged Market Averages in Past 2 Years, Study of Pooled Funds Finds,' *Wall Street Journal*, 28 February 1977.
11. *Ibid.* note 4, p. 28.
12. John Maynard Keynes, *General Theory of Employment, Interest, and Money*, (Harcourt, Brace, & World, New York, 1965).
13. 'Hold That Dart', *Forbes*, 1 October 1973.
14. *Ibid.*
15. Charles Mackay, *Memoirs of Extraordinary Popular*

Delusions and the Madness of Crowds, (Routledge and Sons, London, 1892).

16. Burton G. Malkiel, *A Random Walk Down Wall Street*, (W.W. Norton and Co., New York, 1973), p. 36.

Chapter 5:

1. Origen, *Contra Celsum* 4.67, translated by Henry Chadwick, (Cambridge, 1953).
2. Diogenes Laertius, *Lives of Eminent Philosophers*, translated by Robert D. Hicks (1850-1929), (Heinemann, London, 1942).
3. *Ptolemy's Tetrabiblos*, op. cit.
4. *The Works of Philo Judaeus, the Contemporary of Josephus*, translated from the Greek by C.D. Young, B.A. (Henry G. Bohn., London, 1855).
5. *The History of Herodotus*, translated by G.C. Macaulay, M.A. (MacMillan & Co. Ltd., London, 1914).
6. *Ibid.*, note 4.
7. Francis Barrett, *The Magus*, (London, 1801. Available from The Aquarian Press, Wellingborough).
8. *Complete Works of Tacitus*, translated by A.J. Church and W.J. Brodribb, (Random House, New York, 1942).
9. Eliphas Levi, *Dogme et Rituel de la Haute Magie*, (Editions Niclaus N. Bussiere, Paris, 1977, pp. 334 et seq).
10. *Ibid.*
11. H.P. Blavatsky, *Studies in Occultism*, (The Theosophical University Press, Pasadena, California, undated, p. 185).

Chapter 6:

1. Franz Hartmann, *The Life and the Doctrines of Paracelsus.* (United States Book Company, Boston, 1891).
2. *Ibid.*, p. 225.
3. *Ibid.*, p. 221.
4. *Ibid.*, pp. 221, 310.
5. *Ibid.*, 310.
6. *Ibid.*, p. 254.
7. *Ibid.*, p. 311.
8. *Ibid.*, p. 259.
9. *Ibid.*, p. 310.
10. *Ibid.*, p. 221.

11. *Ibid.*, p. 254.
12. *Ibid.*, p. 251.
13. *Ibid.*, p. 251.
14. *Ibid.*, p. 264.
15. *Ibid.*, p. 215.
16. *Ibid.*, p. 213.
17. *Ibid.*, p. 215.
18. H.P. Blavatsky, *Isis Unveiled*, (The Theosophy Company, Los Angeles, 1968, vol. 1, p. 507).
19. Pierre-Daniel Templier, *Eric Satie*, translated by Elena L. French and David S. French, (The M.I.T. Press, Cambridge, 1969).
20. Hartmann, op. cit., p. 252.
21. *Ibid.*, p. 259.
22. *Ibid.*, p. 244.
23. *Ibid.*, p. 193.
24. *Ibid.*, p. 264.
25. H.P. Blavatsky, *The Secret Doctrine*, (The Theosophical Publishing Company, London, 1888).
26. A.T. Barker, *The Mahatma Letters to A.P. Sinnett*, (The Theosophical Publishing House, Adyar, Madras, 1962, p. 160).
27. H.P. Blavatsky, *Secret Instructions to Probators of an Occult Esoteric School*, (Health Research, Mokelumne Hill, California, 1969, p. 112). These papers are the unedited original instructions of H.P. Blavatsky to the Esoteric Section of the Theosophical Society. They can also be found in heavily edited form in volume three of *The Secret Doctrine*, (The Theosophical Publishing Society, London, 1897).
28. Quoted by Mircea Eliade, *Yoga*. The Princeton University Press, Princeton, 1958.
29. *The Key of Solomon the King*, translated by S.L. MacGregor Mathers (d. 1918), (G. Redway, London, 1889).
30. H.P. Blavatsky, *The Secret Doctrine*, op. cit.
31. Pliny, *Natural History*, (W. Heinemann, Ltd., London) 1938, xviii, pp. 321ff).
32. *Ibid.*
33. H.P. Blavatsky, *The Secret Doctrine*, op. cit.

Chapter 7:

  1. Pliny, *Natural History*. This is also discussed by Blavatsky in *The Secret Doctrine*, and by Arthur Koestler in *The

Sleepwalkers, a History of Man's Changing Vision of the Universe. (The MacMillan Company, New York, 1959, part I, chaper II).

2. Johannes Kepler (1571-1630), *The Harmonies of the World,* translated by Charles Glenn Wallis, volume 16 of *The Great Books of the Western World,* (William Benton, Chicago, 1952, p. 1009).

3. *Ibid.* In *The Sleepwalkers* (p. 33), Arthur Koestler contemptuously refers to Kepler's writing of this book as 'one of the most astonishing episodes in the history of thought, and an antidote to the pious belief that the Progress of Science is governed by logic.'

4. Koestler, op. cit.

5. Serge Hutin, *L'Alchimie,* (Presses universitaires de France, Paris, 1971).

6. The senses-are-responses-to-vibrations theory seems to have first been put forward by C.W. Leadbeater in his *Clairvoyance,* (Theosophical Publishing Society, London, 1899).

7. Hartmann, *Paracelsus,* p. 58n.

8. C.W. Leadbeater, *The Masters and the Path.* (The Theosophical Publishing House, Adyar, 1925).

9. Hartmann, op. cit., p. 288.

10. *Ibid.,* p. 311.

11. *Ibid.*

12. *Ibid.,* p. 297.

13. Hartmann, op. cit.

14. *Ibid.*

15. Paramahansa Yogananda, *The Autobiography of a Yogi,* (Philosophical Society, New York, 1946).

16. Hartmann. op, cit., p. 260.

17. H.P. Blavatsky, *Secret Instructions,* p. 16.

18. Theos Bernard, *Hindu Philosophy,* (The Philosophical Library, New York, 1946).

19. H.P. Blavatsky, *Secret Instructions,* p. 22.

20. *Ibid.,* p. 86.

21. Vyasa, *Bhasya,* translated by James Haughton Woods, *The Yoga System of Patanjali,* (Motilal Banarsidass, Delhi, India, 1977). These theories were discussed at length in my earlier book on *Invisibility.* (The Aquarian Press, Wellingborough, 1982).

22. *Gheranda Samhita*, translated by Srisachandra Vasu, (The Indian Press, Allahabad, 1914). See also *The Yoga Upanishads*, translated by Srinavasa Ayyangar, (The Theosophical Publishing House, Adyar, 1952).

23. W.Y. Evan-Wentz, *The Tibetan Book of the Dead*, (Oxford University Press, 1971).

24. 'Clairvoyance', in Israel Regardie, *The Golden Dawn*, (Llewellyn Publications, Saint Paul, Minnesota, 1974, vol. 4, p. 12).

25. H.P. Blavatsky, 'Practical Occultism', in *Studies in Occultism*, (The Theosophical University Press, Pasadena, California, undated).

26. Regardie, op. cit., p. 99.

27. *Ibid.*, p. 104.

28. *Ibid.*

29. *Ibid.*

30. Mouni Sadhu, *The Tarot*, London: George Allen & Unwin, Ltd., 1962.

31. Rama Prasad, *Nature's Finer Forces*, (The Theosophical Publishing House, Adyar 1933).

32. C.W. Leadbeater, *Man Visible and Invisible*, (The Theosophical Publishing Society, London, 1902).

33. Gammon, *Astrology and the Edgar Cayce Readings*, (The Edgar Cayce Foundation, Virginia Beach, Virginia, 1967).

34. Translated by James Haughton Woods, op. cit.

35. W.Y. Evans-Wentz, *Tibetan Yoga and Secret Doctrines*, (Oxford University Press, 1977).

36. Rama Prasad, op. cit.

37. Hartmann, op. cit.

38. Alfred Gordon Bennett, *Focus On the Unknown*, (Rider, London, 1953).

Chapter 8:

1. Eliphas Levi, *Dogma et Rituel de la Haute Magie*, (Editions Niclaus N. Bussiere, Paris, 1977, p. 152).

Chapter 9:

1. Ralph Houston, *Talk Does Not Cook the Rice*, (Samuel Weiser, New York, 1982).

2. 'Synchronicity and Consciousness', *Membership Research*

Project, (The Association for Research and Enlightenment, Virginia Beach, Virginia, August 1983).

3. 'Results of the August Membership Project – Synchronicity and Consciousness', *Membership Research Project*, (The Association for Research and Enlightenment, Virginia Beach, Virginia, November 1983).

4. 'Results of August and December Projects', *Membership Research Project*, (The Association of Research and Enlightenment, Virginia Beach, April 1984).

5. Sigmund Freud, *The Basic Writings of Sigmund Freud*, translated and edited by Dr. A.A. Brill, (The Modern Library, New York, 1938, pp. 163-4).

6. *Ibid.*, p. 165.

7. Eliphas Levi, *Dogme et Rituel de la Haute Magie*, (Editions Niclaus N. Bussiere, Paris, 1977, p. 311).

8. Israel Regardie, *My Rosicrucian Adventure*, (Llewellyn Publications, Saint Paul, Minnesota, 1971, p. 89).

9. Lafcadio Hearn (1850-1904), *In Ghostly Japan*, (Sampson Low & Co., London, 1899).

Chapter 10:

1. William H. Harrison, *Mother Shipton Investigated*, (Privately Printed, London, 1881).

2. Josephus, *Antiquities* xii.xi.2., and *Wars* 1.111.4. in *Complete Works*, translated by William Whiston, A.M. (Wm. P. Nimmo, Edinburgh, 1867, p. 442).

3. George Carleton, *The Madness of Astrologers*, (W. Turner, London, 1624).

4. Cicero, *De Divinatione*, translated by William A. Falconer, (Wm. Heinemann, London, 1964, XXV, p. 281).

5. Alan Vaughan, *Patterns of Prophecy*, (Dell, New York, 1973, pp. 75-6).

6. Cicero, op. cit., XXIII, p. 275.

7. *Ibid.*, XXIII, pp. 275-277.

8. Diogenes Laertius, *Lives of Eminent Philosophers*, translated by Robert D. Hicks (1850-1929), (Heinemann, London, 1942).

9. Cicero, op. cit., XXV, p. 281.

10. Carl Jung, *Memories, Dreams, Reflections*, translated by Richard and Clara Winston, (Vintage Books, New York, 1963).

11. Francis Bacon, 'On Prophecies', op. cit.
12. Carleton, op. cit., p. 14.
13. *Gentlemen's Magazine*, 1801, Part II, pp. 1094-1095.
14. *Gentlemen's Magazine*, 1822, Part I, p. 311.
15. Sir Nathaniel Wraxall, Bart., *Historical Memoirs of My Own Time, Part the First from 1772 to 1780.* (London, 1815, vol. 1, pp. 313-317).
16. Lord George Gordon Noel Byron, *The Complete Poetical Works of Lord Byron.* (The Riverside Press, Cambridge, Massachusetts, 1933).
17. C.G. Jung, 'Synchronicity: An Acausal Connection Principle', in *The Structure and Dynamics of the Psyche*, translated by R.F.C. Hull, Princeton University Press, Princeton, New Jersey, 1969, p. 422).
18. *Ibid.*, p. 438.
19. *Ibid.*
20. Herodotus, *The History of Herodotus*, translated by G.C. Macaulay, M.A. (MacMillan & Co., Ltd., London 1914, 1.34-44, vol. 1, pp. 16-20).
21. Vaughan, op. cit.
22. Cicero, op. cit. XXVII, p. 285.
23. Eliphas Levi, *Dogme et Rituel de la Haute Magie*, (Editions Niclaus N. Bussiere, Paris, 1977, p. 152).
24. This same instance also applies to Annie Besant, H.P.B.'s disciple. Her horoscope predicted that she would die in 1907, yet she lived until 1933. See Gertrude Leavenworth Marvin Williams, *The Passionate Pilgrim*, (Coward McCann, New York, 1931, p. 266). See also Madame Blavatsky, *Isis Unveiled.* (vol. 2, pp. 563-4).
25. Joseph Weed, *The Wisdom of the Mystic Masters.* (The Parker Publishing Company, West Nyack, New York, 1968, p. 19).
26. 'Sanitarium's [*sic*] Errors Kill a Frenchman, Prescriptions Incorrectly Copied, Filled, and Given to Wrong Man — Six Guilty of Death', 22 February 1928 *New York Times*, p. 5. (Copyright 1928 by The New York Times Company. Reprinted by permission.)
27. *Fama Fratemitatis Rosae Crucis*, printed at Kassel, 1614, translated by Thomas Vaughan in 1652 and reprinted by Arthur Edward Waite in *The Real History of the Rosicrucians*, (The Rudolf Steiner Publishing Company,

Blauvelt, New York, 1977, p. 74). It may be worth mentioning here that this is a reference to the *ancient* Rosicrucians, and not to any of the dozen or so modern organizations which may use that name.

28.   Vyasa, *Bhasya*, translated by James Haughton Woods, *The Yoga System of Patanjali*, Motilal Banarsidass, Delhi, India, 1977, p. 251).

29.   John Aubrey, *Miscellanies*, (A. Bettesworth & J. Bailey, London, 1721).

30.   C.G. Jung, 'The Soul and Death', in *The Interpretation of Nature and the Psyche*, (The Princeton University press, Princeton, 1973, p. 410).

Chapter 11:

1.   'Case Against the Rope', *The Economist* 2-8 July, 1983, p. 12.
2.   Sigmund Freud, 'Some Character Types Met With In Psychoanalytic Work', in *The Standard Edition of the Complete Psychological Works of Sigmund Freud*, translated by James Strachey, in collaboration with Anna Freud, (The Hogarth Press, London, 1953).
3.   *Ibid.*
4.   *Ibid.*

Index